Joanna Thompson

England Calling

Thienemann

Chalk Farm School for Girls

"It's your grandma on the phone, Emily!"

It's 7.34 am. It's *Saturday*. I'm in bed, of course. My mother knows: *it's just too early.* And then my father calls out in German, "Emily, Telefon für dich! Die Queen Mother aus England! Schnell!"

I pull my **blanket** over my head.

I'm Emily Hausmann. I'm 14 years old and I live in Prenzlauer Berg – the coolest part of Berlin, I think – with my father and mother and brother Max, who's nine. He's lucky; he's the only one of us still asleep.

I get shouted at in two languages because my mum's from England and my dad's German, so I'm bilingual, *zweisprachig*. It's cool. I can sing along with pop songs and watch films in English. I get top marks in English at school, too, and my teacher, Herr Eisenhardt, *hates* me because he knows I'm better than him. Ha!

That Saturday morning at 7.34 am, my life hadn't changed yet. It would change forever later, at around 7.46. But at 7.34, things were the same as they'd always been.

+++ blanket – Decke +++

I was still in the same bedroom, its walls covered with pictures of my favourite bands and with pictures that I took. That's my hobby, taking photos. There's so much to photograph in Berlin – great looking boys, **for instance**. My camera's always near my bed. It's an old one that Auntie Nora, my mother's sister, bought in Tokyo years ago. She **passed** it **on** to me and I love it. Nearly as much as I love my bed on Saturday mornings.

My father comes into my room. Sascha Hausmann, 46, writer. I lift my blanket two centimetres or so. He looks bad, grumpy, still in his black pyjamas. He writes late at night and *hates* early morning phone calls. I think sleepily about how much I look like him, how tall we both are, how dark. I've got my mother's light blue eyes, **though**. My grandma's eyes, too, in fact.

My father's not thinking about how much we look **alike**. My father's thinking about how much he wants to go back to bed. "Emily, wach auf! Die wartet schon eine viertel Stunde auf dich! Weißt du, was es kostet, aus England anzurufen?!"

It's still 1978 in my father's **mind**, sometimes. "Ja, Papa," I say. "Es kostet … fünf Cent pro Minute?"

"Egal – deine Grandma ist 82 und in dem Alter zählt jede Sekunde!"

He's right. I fall out of bed. I groan – it *hurts* getting up this early at the weekend.

+++ for instance – zum Beispiel +++ to pass on – weitergeben +++ though – aber, allerdings +++ alike – gleich +++ mind – *hier:* Vorstellung, Kopf

I go to our **hall**, where our telephone is "parked". We must be the only family in the country who still have one **plugged in** at the wall. My father's idea – to stop me living on the phone. It works, I have to say.

My mother's waiting for me. Eleanor Hausmann, 47, school teacher. Small and blonde, I sometimes wish I looked more like her. Not this morning. She looks so tired, poor thing, dark shadows under those eyes of ours.

She gives me the phone, saying: "Remember – she can't hear so well. Shout! And she's very excited about something."

+++ hall – Flur +++ to plug in – einstecken +++

"HELLO, GRANDMA!" I try to shout, but my voice feels like it's asleep, too. "IT'S ME, EMILY. HOW ARE YOU?"

Grandma says, of course, "PARDON?"

My grandma, **bless her**, is my mother's mother, who lives in a big house in the country in England. The house is old and beautiful and nearly the size of my school here. Grandma is **incredible**, too. She gets up at 5 am and still walks into the nearest town (two miles! 3.22 kilometres!) every day. She's a bit **deaf** and other than that – *top fit,* as my father says. We don't see her very often. I think this might be because she doesn't really like my father.

"HOW ARE YOU?" My voice gets louder. My mum puts her hands over her ears and walks away.

"Emily!" my grandmother says happily. "My dear, I have some wonderful news."

It's now 7.46. Grandma starts to tell me the news that will change my life.

"Do you remember you said you wanted to go to school in England?"

I didn't quite say that. I think I said that it MIGHT be "fun" or "cool" to live in England for a bit one day. I don't remember **mentioning** anything about wanting to go to school there.

But I say, "YES, GRANDMA."

"Well, I met my dear friend Mildred last week. Her

+++ bless her – Gott schütze sie +++ incredible – unglaublich +++ deaf – schwerhörig, taub +++ to mention – erwähnen +++

granddaughter goes to Chalk Farm School and there's a place free in her class because one poor girl got …"

Here, **actually**, I stop listening 1) because I'm so sleepy and 2) because Grandma is *always* talking about Chalk Farm School for Girls. It's the school, a **boarding school** actually, where she went. It's right in the centre of London and she can talk for hours, days and *weeks* about how exciting her life there was. She has *hundreds* of photos of her school days; my father always runs away when she gets them out. Maybe this is why she doesn't like him.

My mother went to Chalk Farm School for Girls, too. She doesn't talk about how exciting her life there was. She talks about how *boring* her life there was because there were no boys. Yes, you heard right. *None. Zero. Null.*

"Then I had the idea!" shouts Grandma.

"What idea?" I wake up.

"That you should go to Chalk Farm, too!!!"

Now I'm *really* awake. My grandma then says more things like – *great family tradition* **and so on**, but I stop listening again. She talks and talks until finally I say to her, "Grandma, thanks a lot. Can I think about it?" I put the phone down and I run back to bed. I lie there and think about the Queen Mother's offer. *Think, think, think* …

I also *think, think, think* about how much I like my

+++ actually – sogar, eigentlich +++ boarding school – Internat +++ and so on – und so weiter +++

life here in Berlin, about my friends and school and Sebastian Junger, the love of my life so far. Then I try to remember the first time I went to England, when I was four or so. **Even though** I was so young, London took my breath away.

And then I fall back to sleep.

When I finally get out of bed again, two hours later, my parents are waiting. I realise that my grandma hasn't told them about her idea, so I tell them.

They're surprised.

"Chalk Farm School!" says my mum. "Oh!"

I can see she's remembering all the bad things she told me about it. About how having no boys around made the girls there totally boy crazy. "That's great!" she says quickly. *Too quickly*. "What a great chance! London, it's a wonderful city!"

My father smiles. "Du denkst jetzt bestimmt an all diese Geschichten, die dir Mama erzählt hat … Wie schrecklich das war im Internat …"

My mother gives him a look. One of her schoolteacher looks. Scary. My father goes red.

"Ich denke grad an ziemlich viel, Papa," I say, a bit dramatically.

It's true. This is very serious **stuff**. I have a nice life here in Berlin. I've got lovely friends. My two best ones are Betti Kremp and Merle Appel and we love to sit in Mondstein, a café (our café!) at the corner of Kas-

+++ even though – obwohl +++ stuff – Sachen, Zeug +++

tanienallee and Oderbergerstraße on Saturdays and drink *Milchkaffee* and watch the world of Prenzlauer Berg go by. All the beautiful people, all their cool clothes.

And if we forget about Herr Eisenhardt for a moment, I really like my school, the Hermann-Hesse-Gymnasium, too. I'm in the *achte Klasse* and the best thing about the *achte Klasse*, by a long way, is Sebastian Junger. I always try to sit behind him so I can watch him, secretly. It means looking at the back of his neck a lot. Luckily, this is a very lovely **sight**.

Even my parents are … OK. It could be worse, my mother always tells me, and she's right. They're **pretty** cool. My dad's a writer, which means he's home a lot and never has any money. Mum's a teacher, meaning she's at home a lot, too, in the school holidays and that she has a little bit more money. But only a little bit.

She came to Germany to study years ago, met my father and never went back to England. My dad likes to joke about her being an English princess and how she gave up the good life to be with him, in the bad/poor life. That's why he calls Grandma the Queen Mother. Grandma has money. We don't normally see much of it, as my dad often **complains**.

So Grandma offering to pay for me to go to an expensive boarding school in London is a surprise. "She's getting old," says my mother, looking sad.

+++ sight – Anblick, Blick +++ pretty – ziemlich +++ to complain – sich beschweren +++

Then she smiles. “Emily, it’d be the chance of a lifetime. It really is a great school, you know. It would be wonderful for your English.”

“I speak English!” I say, **offended**!

“I know, I know, but really to *live* a language is something different.”

“I like things here,” I say quietly.

“I know you do. But they’ll still be here when you get back. We won’t run away, will we, Dad?”

My parents have always spoken English to each other. My dad **winks** at me. “Och … Wahrscheinlich nicht.”

+++ offended – verletzt, beleidigt +++ to wink – zwinkern +++

Notfall!

Should I stay or should I go? The words of an old rock song my parents sometimes play. It's my question now. How to decide what to do? There's only one way; *Milchkaffee* at High Noon. I send an **urgent** text message to Betti and Merle: *Mondstein um 12? Notfall!*

Usually, *Notfall* means one thing – either boy trouble or hot boy news! So when Betti and Merle arrive, they're a little red-faced and **breathless**. They think they're going to hear about Sebastian – that he has finally asked me out on a date, perhaps.

When I tell them **instead** about my grandmother offering to send me to London, they are – *gobsmacked*, my mother would call it. *Verblüfft*, my father would say.

Merle looks like she might cry. Merle cries very easily, at anything, really. Pictures of Knut the *Eisbär*, silly Top Model shows on TV. Sometimes at my photos of us together. Anything. Merle says it's because she's red-haired and redheads are more emotional. Betti says it's because Merle's *neurotisch*.

+++ urgent – dringend +++ breathless – atemlos +++ instead – stattdessen +++

Merle starts to speak. "Aber was ist mit …?" But then she has to stop because she really *is* crying.

Betti, the most organised of the three of us, always has a pack of *Tempos* with her. She passes one to Merle, silently, staring at me as she does so. Betti's really pretty but she can look hard. Boys are scared of her, sometimes. *I'm* scared of her, sometimes. Now, for instance.

Betti takes a **sip** of her *Milchkaffee*. She **glances** quickly **at** a cute blonde boy who walks past and then finally says: "Das ist eine super Chance! Du *musst* gehen, keine Frage! Du wärst bescheuert, es nicht zu machen, und würdest es dein ganzes Leben bereuen!"

Then – surprise – Merle speaks, too. She sounds a bit as though she is talking underwater or from inside a wooden box, but I *think* she says: "Betti hat recht! So eine Chance kriegt man wirklich nur einmal im Leben."

Well, that was easy. I'm a bit sad, actually. It seems like everyone who knows me is very pleased that I might leave them. **Including** my parents. They're trying not to show it, but I can *feel* it. My little brother Max was openly **ecstatic** – *Yippee! Can I have your bedroom?*

And now my best friends, too … am I so awful?

Merle **reaches over** to take my hand. Her eyes are still red. "Emily, wir lieben dich und du wirst uns echt fehlen …" Her voice starts to shake, dangerously. "Für ein Jahr, sagst du?" She **bursts into tears** again.

+++ sip – Schluck +++ to glance at – einen Blick werfen auf +++ including – eingeschlossen +++ ecstatic – begeistert +++ to reach over – die Hand herüberstrecken +++ +++ to burst into tears – in Tränen ausbrechen +++

Betti passes Merle another *Tempo*, still without looking at her, and says, calmly: "Reiß dich zusammen, Mädel. Ein Jahr. Und wir können Emily zwischendurch besuchen!"

Now I feel like crying as well and even Betti looks away, up at the sky, which is blue and hopeful today.

It's my turn to reach out to Merle. In fact, I give her a big **hug**. Then I say, "Eine Sache muss ich euch noch erzählen … Es gibt keine Jungs da!"

Merle stops crying and Betti's eyes get bigger. In shocked stereo Merle says, "Keine Jungs???!!!" and Betti **gasps**, "*Gar* keine?" I shake my head. I can see this has changed things for them.

Merle looks confused. "Aber in England gibt es doch Jungs! Wir haben diese zwei aus, wo war das, aus Leeds oder so letztes Jahr bei der Popkomm kennengelernt. Die waren beide soooo süß …"

Betti rolls her eyes. "Merle, mein Schatz, natürlich gibt's in *England* Jungs. Emily meinte nur, dass das Internat, wo die Queen Mother sie hinschicken will, eine Mädchenschule ist."

Merle **squeals** and puts her hand over her mouth. Her face says – *how* ***disgusting!*** You would think I had just told her I was off to *Dschungelcamp* to eat worms for twelve months.

"So was … gibt's in echt? Ich dachte … das gab's nur in Geschichten. Vor dem Krieg oder so."

+++ hug – Umarmung +++ to gasp – japsen +++ to squeal – einen Schrei ausstoßen +++ disgusting – ekelhaft +++

"Na ja," I smile, "meine Mutter war auch auf dieser Schule. Sie fand es schrecklich ohne Jungs. Jetzt meinte sie natürlich, dass das alles doch nicht so schlimm gewesen sei …"

Merle **beams**. "Und guck mal! Sie hat einen super Typen kennengelernt! Dein Papa ist doch süß!"

Betti looks serious. "Aber sie musste dafür nach Deutschland ziehen, Merle. Weil es keine Männer in England gibt!"

And we all laugh until Merle looks like she'll cry again.

She doesn't cry, because she has to leave. Merle has three, count them, younger brothers and sisters and she has *Super-Nanny-Dienst,* as she calls it, today. "Betet für mich," she **groans**. She **heads off** to get the tram **a couple of** stops to where she lives. Six people, three bedrooms. Merle's life's not easy. Maybe that's *really* why she cries so much.

Betti lives near me, so we walk home together. She's an **only child** and her parents let her do her own thing, **pretty much**. We're in no hurry. We don't talk. Both of us are trying to imagine life without each other.

We walk past the *Fotoautomat* near the top of Kastanienallee, the one which takes black and white photos. It's always busy, lots of tourists, but today, strangely, there's no one. It's then I realise I don't have

+++ to beam – strahlen +++ to groan – stöhnen +++
to head off – losziehen +++ a couple of – einige +++ pretty much – *hier*: weitgehend +++ only child – Einzelkind +++

my camera with me. I was so excited about meeting Merle and Betti that I forgot it. Suddenly I feel I want to remember today, Berlin in the sun, because I know, somehow, things will change soon.

So I say to Betti, "Komm! Ich brauch ein Andenken von heute!" And we get in and make silly faces for the camera as the *Fotoautomat* POPS! and **FLASHES**! at us.

As we wait outside for the pictures, Betti asks quietly, "Und was ist mit Sebastian?"

It's a fine question. Sebastian Junger, the boy I've loved now for a year. Half of that time in secret and half … openly but hopelessly. Sebastian only has eyes for beautiful but *zickig* (Betti's word) Katharina

+++ to flash – blitzen +++

Müller, who's also in our class. Unfortunately. Katharina can't quite decide whether she wants Sebastian or not. She plays with him, we all think.

We all think he likes me a lot, too. Betti has a brilliant system for checking how interested a boy is in you – *Bettis Top-Liebestest* we call it – and it's pure **genius.** It's a list of questions about how a boy behaves with you. *Does his face* **light up** *when he sees you? Does he ignore his mobile phone when he's with you? Does he actually listen to what you say?* Things like that. Sebastian scores a 7, which means, **roughly**, and I'm **quoting** here: *Er sieht dich nur als eine gute Freundin – aber gib die Hoffnung nicht auf …*

The pictures come out of the machine. I pick them up carefully. We look really funny.

"Ach, Sebastian", I say **casually**. "Schauen wir mal. Das wäre doch der Super-Liebestest oder? Ob er überhaupt reagiert, wenn ich sage, dass ich für ein Jahr nach London fahre."

I play it cool with Betti but actually I spend all of Sunday trying to imagine what Sebastian might say about me going away. I see him, on his knees, **begging** me not to leave. *Du bist die Richtige für mich! Katharina ist so … oberflächlich! Ich war so blöd, so blind, Liebling … Aber London wartet auf mich,* I say. *Ich muss gehen!* And then, in my fantasy, we have our own final sum-

+++ genius – Genialität +++ to light up – aufleuchten +++ roughly – ungefähr +++ to quote – zitieren +++ casual – beiläufig, lässig +++ to beg – bitten, flehen +++

mer of love, walking hand-in-hand in the park, eating ice cream, going to concerts and museums. Finally it's time. Sebastian takes me to the airport to put me on the plane to London. He's trying not to cry. We kiss and say goodbye. But I can't do it! I change my mind and run towards him, shouting: *Ich kann dich nicht verlassen!*

That was the fantasy. The reality was, of course, a bit different.

Monday morning always means, **yuck**, English with Herr Eisenhardt. You might remember me telling you that Herr Eisenhardt doesn't exactly love me: Mondays are normally traumatic for both of us. But today he actually looks quite **jolly**. He comes **whistling** into class. He even smiles at me. And then I realise: *He knows I'm going away*. My parents phoned the school last week to tell them.

"Emily! You're leaving us!" he says in English. "Off to London ... how wonderful!"

Everyone in class turns to look at me, including Sebastian. This wasn't quite the way I'd planned for him to find out but, well, too late now.

Sebastian looks ... *really happy for me*. It's my worst **nightmare**.

Someone else is *really happy for me*. And for himself. "All the very best," says Herr Eisenhardt. He laughs again.

+++ yuck – ätzend +++ jolly – fröhlich +++ to whistle – pfeifen +++ nightmare – Albtraum +++

When the class is finished – for once, I say nothing – I'm getting my things together when Sebastian comes over to me. My heart does that strange thing it always does when he's near. Sometimes it feels like the *click!* that my camera makes when I take a picture.

"Hi, Emily, wie geht's?" he says, smiling. And *click!* goes my heart again.

Sebastian. How to tell you why I love him. He's sporty, without being really, well, *sporty*. He's smart and funny and **modest**. His eyes are **moss** green, his hair dark like the … oh, I could talk about him for hours, but then I'll *really* never get to London so I won't.

"Ist das wirklich wahr? Du fährst nach England ins Internat? Das ist doch super! Glückwunsch!"

At that very moment, I *know* I'm going to London. There's no **doubt** now. *Glückwunsch.* I look at him, closely. I'm trying to see if there's anything behind that word, whether he's … crying *inside* maybe???

Nothing. Sebastian smiles at me, **evenly**. He doesn't say anything about me being the girl for him or how blind or stupid he's been. *Nothing.*

It gets worse because just then Katharina Müller walks past. **Glamorous**, tall as a Redwood tree, blonde-haired and just *horrible*. She has a new leather jacket, I see. Brown. Very **boho** chic. Her dad is some big

+++ modest – bescheiden +++ moss – Moos +++ doubt – Zweifel +++ even – ruhig +++ glamorous – schön, glamourös +++ boho – ausgefallen +++

lawyer, as she tells us *all the time*, and she always has expensive clothes.

She stops and smiles at Sebastian. Sebastian goes white. He only has eyes for her; I'm **invisible**.

Katharina can still see me. Unfortunately. She laughs, the way that witches in films laugh. Her laughter actually *echoes*. "Eine *Mädchenschule*, hab ich gehört. Super! *Jungenwüste*, oder! Ist doch ideal für dich!"

Sebastian laughs, too. He's looking at Katharina in ... *the same way I look at him.*

I'm bright red but I manage to say, "Die Schule ist super und es gibt auch Jungs." But Katharina's already gone, leaving only the smell of her sickly perfume for me to talk to.

I won't miss Katharina Müller, that's for sure. And if Sebastian wants her, well, how great can he really be? He's dying to follow her now, I can tell. He smiles again and says something like, "Aber du schickst mir doch ab und zu mal eine Mail ... Die Adresse hast du, oder?" and then he's gone.

Clunk! goes my heart.

+++ lawyer – Anwalt/Anwältin +++ invisible – unsichtbar +++

The Best School in the World

Luckily, I've a lot to do before I leave so I'm not too sad about Sebastian. I don't think about him *all* the time.

First things first. When planning a trip, Auntie Nora once told me, the most important thing a girl needs is a good suitcase. As mine is not "good" and is, in fact, "bad" (It has a picture of *Winnie Puh* on it, OK?) maybe I could steal the really nice red **vintage** one that I know Merle has?

Even though it's only May and I won't leave until early September, I call Merle. I can hardly hear her above the sound of her hundreds of brothers and sisters screaming, but yes, she shouts, she'll let me take her red 1970's suitcase. Cool. **In return,** I'm to send her something just as cool from England. "Einer dieser Jungs aus Leeds als Briefsendung wäre toll!" she laughs.

Then – oops! – I remember I still have to phone my grandmother and tell her that I would like to go to an expensive girls boarding school in London for a year. Thanks very much.

+++ first things first – eins nach dem anderen +++
vintage – altmodisch, retro +++ in return – als Gegenleistung +++

She doesn't seem surprised. "I knew you would say yes," she screams. "The best school in the world!"

"How can the best school in the world have no boys, Grandma?" I say quietly. So that she can't hear me. Loudly, I say, "GREAT."

Grandma's a fast worker. I get a letter the very next week from Chalk Farm School.

"Dear Emily," it says, "We are very happy to hear that you will be coming to **join** us next **term**. We are sure that you will enjoy …"

But I don't finish reading the letter because there's a brochure with it, all about the school. It's full of pictures of girls … wearing uniforms!

Uniforms. Of course. It's *England.* Die Insel. Alcatraz, it seems, looking at these pictures. I feel sick. The Chalk Farm School uniform is … burgundy ("Weinrot!" I can already hear Katharina Müller screaming) with *yellow* stripes. I look at the pictures of girls in **woollen** jackets, in skirts, short and nylon, and my skin starts to **itch**. It really *does.*

Then I look at my own beautiful pair of black **skinny jeans**, which I wear all the time. If my legs could cry, they would. *No!* they seem to shout. (They really *do.*) And, even worse, the smiling – smiling! – girls in the photos are wearing … **ties.**

Ties. Ties can be cool. I've got a thin black one that

+++ to join – sich jmdm. anschließen +++ term – Halbjahr +++ woollen – aus Wolle +++ to itch – jucken +++ skinny jeans – Röhrenjeans +++ tie – Krawatte +++

I sometimes wear with my red shirt and white jeans, a nice kind of 80s retro look. One of my favourite looks, in fact. But these ties have burgundy and yellow stripes. They're fashion *death. Not for all the money in the world*, I decide.

Suddenly I imagine I can hear Katharina Müller laughing again. It's so real that I actually turn my head.

I sit and stare at the brochure some more. I feel **doomed**. I can't stop looking at it, at the poor, smiling girls in the pictures. Can't anyone help them? Betti's mum writes letters *gegen Folter und so* for Amnesty International, maybe they could ...

My mother comes into the room. She's smiling and carrying some books from school, which she drops loudly when she sees my face. "Emily!" she screams. "Darling ... what's wrong?"

I can't speak so I just **point at** the brochure. She looks confused.

"Uniforms," I gasp. "Bad uniforms ..."

Mum bursts out laughing. "Oh, the *uniform!* You know, it hasn't changed a bit since my days. I think it was even the same when your grandmother went there."

She sees my face. "I mean," she says quickly, "I'm sure it's not as itchy ... modern **fabrics**. You won't sweat, not as much as we did ..."

I repeat – *Itchy. Sweat. Unchanged in 70 years.* **No way**, baby.

+++ doomed – verloren +++ to point at – zeigen auf +++ fabric – Stoff +++ no way – nie im Leben +++

"I'm not wearing a uniform," I shout. "No! I'll look … awful. Everyone will laugh at me."

My mum's suddenly serious. "No, Emily, they won't. The great thing about uniforms is that everyone looks the same and actually that's really nice. Makes you feel that you're part of the same team …"

I'm listening really hard, honestly, and I am feeling a bit better. But then my mother turns to another page in the brochure. "Look! Hockey. You know, I was actually in the hockey team! I wasn't bad, maybe you'll be like me."

My mother must've dropped her **brain** with her books when she came in. I do not *do* sport. I mean, I'm

+++ brain – Gehirn +++

not lazy and I love to walk, for instance (I also forgot to mention – I'm not bad at table tennis), but anything that makes you *sweat* – nasty word – is not me.

The room's **spinning**. Strange sports, bad uniforms … could it be any worse? It could be. It is. My mother's still smiling her way through the brochure, making the same kinds of noises she does when she looks at old baby photos … *oooh! awwhhh!*

"Oooh! awwhhh!" she **coos**. "The **dorms**! I wonder who you'll get to **bunk with**?"

Dorms? Bunk with? I thought I spoke English. Actually, I thought English was my mother tongue until tonight. What *is* she talking about?

"Emily. Look at the picture."

My mother used to teach English in our house when my brother and me were small, before she went back to work at school. She had one student, a very kind but rather slow old lady who always brought *Kinder Überraschungseier* for my brother and me. I can still remember hearing my mother trying to teach her the same things over and over again. *This is a pen. That is a table.*

"This is a *dorm*, Emily," she says, in the same voice.

Dorm would seem to mean *Gefängniszelle* in German. A grey-looking room with lots of beds that appear to be made of stone. *Nice*. There are pretty teenage girls, once again, lying about on the beds,

+++ to spin – sich drehen +++ to coo – *hier:* ausrufen +++ dorm – Schlafsaal +++ to bunk with – sich mit jmdm. den Schlafsaal teilen +++

smiling as if they were Paris Hilton waiting for room service in one of her daddy's five-star hotels. (What *do* they pay these girls?)

"You mean … we *share* a room???" I gasp, horrified.

My mother looks shocked. "But of course," she says. "That's the fun of it!"

I don't know what I thought a boarding school would be like. I **suppose** I'd never really thought very much about it. When my mother and grandma talked about Chalk Farm School for Girls, I did sometimes think – how *strange* not to live with your family! (Sometimes after a big fight with my parents or Max, of course, I thought: how *great* not to live with your family!)

I never imagined that boarding school was *really* like a hotel or anything but I did **assume** that … well, I'd have my own room.

Mum smiles, lost in sweet Chalk Farm memories. "You can talk all night with the other girls."

Yeah, talk about the best way to make large fires to burn your uniforms in.

Just then, my father comes home with Max. They've been at football. Max is still over-excited, running round our flat, kicking anything he can. My father reads the school's letter, too, and then almost falls on the floor when he sees how much my year at Chalk Farm School for Girls will cost.

+++ to suppose – glauben, vermuten +++ to assume – annehmen +++

"Wir könnten dafür ein Auto kaufen und alle vier nach Australien reisen …" he gasps. He sinks into a chair.

"What did you think, Sascha?" says Mum **patiently**. "Did you think living in England was cheap?"

Mum knows Dad doesn't think England is "cheap". They've been married for nearly 18 years and **at some point** during every one of those 18 years, Dad, I'm sure, has complained about the price of *something* in England. He nearly died the last time we went to a restaurant in England and he saw the bill. But my mother's question makes us all think about money. My grandmother will cover my flight, the school **fees** and my uniform (thanks Grandma!). But there's still the question of pocket money.

My mother and father told the Queen Mother that they'd give me this, and I know they want to feel like they're paying something for this year, too. But all the girls at Chalk Farm School – they'll come from rich families, won't they? We're not rich. Not at all.

My father says what I already knew. "Emily, allzu viel Taschengeld wirst du nicht bekommen, das weißt du, oder? Ich meine, wir könnten dir schon ein bisschen mehr geben, als du hier kriegst …"

Here I get seven euros a week. My mother **takes a deep breath**: "We'll try to make it ten pounds a week."

"Thanks," I say. I mean it. I know that's quite a lot

+++ patient – geduldig +++ at some point – irgendwann +++ fee – Gebühr +++ to take a deep breath – tief Luft holen +++

for them at the moment. My dad hasn't actually earned any money for a long time. He looks a bit **guilty**, I think, sitting in his favourite chair, sad.

I go over to him. I sit on the chair, too. The chair **wobbles** a bit – like a lot of our furniture, it's old. We bought it at the Sunday **flea market** in Mauerpark, near where we live. That's another thing I'll miss.

I put my arms around my dad's neck. "Papa, ist doch kein Problem! Soooo viel Taschengeld brauche ich gar nicht. Keine Sorge!"

He kisses me. "Ach, Emily," he smiles. "Du bist super." And then, because he's my dad, he adds, "Meistens."

He's more serious again now: "Aber dir ist klar, dass das keine normale Schule ist, oder? Dahin gehen nur die wirklich Reichen ... Eigentlich wäre es mir lieber, wenn du auf eine ganz normale Schule gehen würdest, um ein bisschen *echtes* englisches Leben kennenzulernen ..."

My mother, who's been busy trying to stop Max from using her handbag as a football, comes over to join us.

"Your dad's right, Emily," she says slowly. "There will be a lot of very rich girls there. But it doesn't mean that they'll be nasty or **snobbish**."

My father **coughs**.

"It doesn't," my mother says sharply. "Some of them

+++ guilty – schuldbewusst +++ to wobble – wackeln +++ flea market – Flohmarkt +++ snobbish – hochnäsig +++ to cough – husten +++

might be, but there will also be a lot of nice girls there who come from normal families like you, I'm sure of it."

My father isn't. "Noch ist es nicht zu spät, Schatz, es dir anders zu überlegen ..." he begins.

I was wrong, actually: my parents aren't very happy about me leaving. They're not planning wild parties while I'm away. I see that they're a bit scared and – yes, really! – *sad* about losing me for a year.

"Bist du sicher, dass du das machen willst, Emily? Wir wollen keinen Druck auf dich ausüben."

Suddenly I see a lot of pictures, snapshots of everyone I love here in front of my eyes. Mum and Dad and Max and Merle and Betti and Sebastian (even Katharina Müller, for some reason. What's *she* doing in there?).

And then I see London, a big poster-sized panorama shot in my mind: I remember how exciting it all was when I was there. **I think of it all waiting** to be explored and photographed. I remember the cute boys we met from England last year ...

I say simply, "Ja, Papa. Ich bin mir wirklich sicher."

+++ I think of it all waiting ... – I denke daran, wie das alles darauf wartet ... +++

Hurrah for the Organisationskönigin!

Time flies and soon I'll have to fly as well. The school holidays in Germany come and go. Suddenly it's August and nearly time to leave for England. School starts there at the beginning of September.

I pack, finally. *Finally*. Merle's case sits lonely and empty under my bed for months before Betti, always the *Organisationskönigin,* says firmly, "Mach bloß nicht alles auf den letzten Drücker! Das ist viel zu stressig."

She's right, so I sit up till midnight two days before I leave, trying to decide what the most important things in my life are. It's a nightmare. *Pack me! Pack me!* everything in my bedroom seems to say.

Keep a cool head, Emily! I'll get all my school clothes in London. And, really, what does a girl actually *need*? I decide quickly: my black and grey skinny jeans, a few tops, my camera, my Arafat **scarf**, my favourite photos – oops, one of Sebastian at Sports Day just slipped in there! – my iPod …

My whole life in Berlin looks up at me from inside Merle's red case. I close the **lid**.

+++ scarf – Schal +++ lid – Deckel +++

But I can't really close the lid on things here before I've had a going away party, can I? No one's said anything about it.

Everyone is *totally* busy – *mit der Schule und so* – this week. Even Betti doesn't seem to have arranged anything. *Nicht alles auf den letzten Drücker machen,* she said. *Frechheit.*

Well, who needs a party anyway? But as I sit in front of the TV with Max, I'm a bit **heavy of heart**. I can't believe that I'm going to spend my last night in Berlin watching *Gute Zeiten, Schlechte Zeiten* and *Wer wird Millionär.* Then the doorbell rings.

When I open the door, Betti and Merle are standing

+++ to be heavy of heart – schwermütig sein +++

there. They're both wearing grey T-shirts. On the front of each it says: "BERLIN LOVES YOU, EMILY."

Betti pushes another T-shirt, mine, into my hands, says, "Hol mal schnell deinen Fotoapparat!" When I have it, she **grabs** me and pulls me out of the door. *Entführt!*

I've no idea where they're taking me. We go to the U-Bahn – not Mondstein, then. After three stops, at Alexanderplatz, Merle says, "Bitte alle aussteigen."

Now I *am* confused. We walk *really* slowly across Alex. Merle and Betti seem to want to look at *everything* – the *Brunnen der Völkerfreundschaft,* the *Weltuhr*. Merle even wants to admire a display of Playmobil in the windows of Kaufhof ... *ooh, guck mal, Piraten!* Finally it's clear: we're going to the TV Tower!

"Na ja," says Betti, **shrugging her shoulders**. "Wo will man sonst den letzten Abend in Berlin verbringen, wenn nicht auf dem Fernsehturm?"

Brilliant. I see the tower every day, part of the background of my life, but I haven't actually been up it since I was a little girl. Betti and Merle pay and then we all get in the lift, excited, and **zoom up** ...

The doors open at the top and I see them almost **at once**, looking at all the plastic TV towers in the gift shop: Mum and Dad and Max, wearing the same "BERLIN LOVES YOU, EMILY" T-shirts. (Now I know why we had to hang around looking in shop

+++ to grab – greifen, schnappen +++ to shrug one's shoulders – mit der Schulter zucken +++ to zoom up – hinaufsurren +++ at once – sofort +++

windows for so long – to give them enough time to get up before us!) There are three more friends from school, too, Lucy, Maren and Jenny, all smiling. Maren's holding a red rose.

Before I have a chance to look for him, Betti says quickly, "Sebastian hab ich gar nicht gefragt. Frauenabend ... nur dein Papa und Max sind erlaubt."

"Ehrenfrauen, eh, Max?" Dad jokes and everyone laughs.

We go to the table that Betti has booked in the Telecafé – hurrah for the *Organisationskönigin!* Then we eat and drink and look down at our city, all the little lights **twinkling** at us. *Bye bye Emily!* they seem to say. BERLIN LOVES YOU.

I take a few photos of us all, sitting at Table 14 (my age!) and laughing and making a few silly German-English toasts: "Auf London!" "To Berlin!" "Ladies and Gentlemen – the Queen Mother!"

When we finally all come down from the top much later, everyone keeps their *bye bye Emilys* very quick.

No one, not even Merle, wants to cry tonight.

My flight to London is at 10 the following morning, so at 7.30, Mum, Dad, Max and me get into the supersized taxi Dad has ordered for us and go to the airport.

The idea of getting on a plane today without the rest of my family is a bit strange. But it was my choice: I asked my parents *not* to come to London with me. In

+++ to twinkle – funkeln +++

fact, I *begged* them. I offered them **cash**. I had a feeling that I should do this alone, that this year in London should be *mine*.

My mother only agreed when Auntie Nora said she'd pick me up at the airport. I'm to stay with her tonight and we'll meet Grandma at Broughton's, the uniform shop, tomorrow. Then the three of us will go to Chalk Farm School for Girls together – easy.

I'm quite happy at the idea of seeing the Queen Mother again but I'm *really* excited about seeing Auntie Nora. She's a photographer for a big newspaper in England and super cool. There is *nowhere* she hasn't

+++ cash – Bargeld +++

been. She has a two-room flat in an area of London called Fitzrovia. To be honest, I did hope at first that maybe I could live there instead of at school. But my mother reminded me that there were two problems with this idea: 1) Nora travels all the time, and 2) the flat is the same size as my old *Barbie Puppenhaus*.

I check-in, using my British passport (I have two, a British one and a German one). Then – *oh no!* – it's time for more goodbyes.

Here's how they go. Mum makes me promise *five hundred* times that I'll call her and Dad when I get to Nora's place. I've a funny feeling that Mum doesn't really trust my auntie to remember to be at the airport.

And then Mum says something I wasn't expecting. She says, looking very serious, "Remember, it doesn't matter which house you're in."

Mum's spent so long talking to me seriously that Dad and Max only have time to say a quick "Tschüss! Alles Gute!" before I have to **rush** …

I'm on my way.

Once in my seat in the half-empty plane, I think about what Mum said. *It doesn't matter which house you're in.*

I know all about the house system, of course. Oh, yes indeed. The house is the group that you're in at school and there are four at Chalk Farm School for Girls, all named after parts of London – Westminster, Kensington, Bloomsbury and Knightsbridge. The

+++ to rush – sich beeilen +++

Queen Mother was in Kensington House – in 1438 or whenever she was there – meaning that both her daughters should have been in Kensington, too. My mother was. Nora wasn't.

"The Battle of the Houses" is a legend in our family. The Queen Mother talks about it with more emotion than she does about World War II. Nora didn't want to be in Kensington because everyone there was sport crazy. She wanted to be in Bloomsbury House where they did more art. So there was a big fight before my aunt said she wouldn't go to Chalk Farm School *at all* if she couldn't go to Bloomsbury. She won – and broke the Queen Mother's heart.

And I haven't even *thought* about it. Am I to be in Kensington House because of Mum and Grandma? Or do I follow Nora?

I decide to forget about the House question for now. There are more important things to think about like ... trying to decide which perfume I'd choose from the **in-flight magazine** if, say, I had more than ten pounds a week pocket money. Ten pounds, I think sadly, it won't buy me a bottle of **tap** water in Britain, never mind perfume.

In an hour and a half we're there. My other home. My new home. We land **smoothly**, my red bag is the first to arrive, I **flash** my British passport again – everything's going like a dream. Now, I just have to

+++ in-flight magazine – Bordzeitschrift +++
tap – Wasserhahn +++ smooth – sanft +++
to flash – *hier:* schnell zeigen +++

find Nora. I wonder if she'll be wearing that **gorgeous** Prada coat she has …

I look at all the people standing around in the arrivals hall, some holding signs with strange names. I look behind them. I look in the coffee shop. None of them are wearing Prada coats. None of them are Nora.

I **sigh**. I'm not really surprised, but it would have been nice … and my mum will **chop** her up into tiny Prada pieces if she finds out.

Don't panic. I try to think what Betti would do. It works – I hear Betti's voice as clearly as if she were there. *Bleib cool. Mach dein Handy an. Kauf dir eine tolle Zeitschrift und trink einen Cappuccino.*

So I switch my phone on. I try to call Nora but there's only her mailbox. I open my purse and get out the pounds that my mum gave me. I look at them carefully. A five pound note is a blue Queen, ten pounds is a brown Queen.

I buy a copy of a magazine with my favourite band in it. I order a cappuccino and a delicious looking piece of cake in the first café I find … one brown Queen, gone already.

I'm just wondering if I should get another expensive coffee – twice the price of Mondstein *Milchkaffee!* – when I finally see Auntie Nora running into the lounge. She *is* wearing that Prada coat, the pink-and-black one. She looks great, coat and long blonde hair flying, but she's very stressed. She's an hour late!

+++ gorgeous – wunderschön, prachtvoll +++
to sigh – seufzen +++ to chop – hacken +++

She rushes over and throws her arms around me.

"Sorry," she says, about 20 times. "I was stuck in traffic … my mobile battery was **flat**." She looks around as though we're being watched and then almost whispers, "Please don't tell your mum."

"No way." I shake my head. I mean it.

Nora laughs. "That's my girl! Come on then, London's waiting!"

She grabs my luggage trolley with Merle's case on it. "Cute bag!" she says, smiling.

+++ flat – *hier:* leer +++

The School across the Street

Nora has a great car, a vintage 1973 Citroen. It looks cool but it's a big mess inside, worse than Max's bedroom. It's full of Nora's life, camera bags, posters, old coffee cups and – very strange this – a big dog's bed (Nora doesn't have a dog.)

I open the door and *phew!* it smells like 50 dogs have been living there since about ... 1973.

I fight my way into the car, pushing the dog's bed off the front seat. "I looked after my friend's Newfoundland for a few weeks," says Nora, seeing my face. "Benjy. Great dog."

It takes us about two hours to get across London. Nora likes to play music *loud* so it's a bit like talking to the Queen Mother – I have to shout. And when I'm not shouting, I'm looking out of the window ... I'm here in London, it's so exciting.

We finally arrive in Fitzrovia. I like this part of London a lot. It's really central, near Oxford Street and Regent's Park. Nora even has her own *Fernsehturm* in her street, the Telecom Tower. I take some photos of the tower and of Nora standing outside her flat.

Then we **puff** our way up to the fifth floor. Nora's flat really is even smaller than I remember it. Tiny. I call my mother straight away to tell her I'm OK. "Nora picked you up alright, no problems?" Mum asks **suspiciously**. "No problems," I say.

After I've finished with Mum, Nora **mutters,** "I'm not very good with my cooker!" and orders us some curry from an Indian restaurant nearby. It's much spicier than the curry in Germany and it's delicious. Nora tells me about all her travels and her favourite places while we eat.

She tells me she's off again on Monday, to Madrid this time, to cover a big story there. We look at a **stack** of her photos – from Pakistan, Vietnam, New Zealand – and I show her some of my pictures from Berlin and well, *Berlin*, which she's **nice about**.

And then she **hands** me something. It's a purple book – an album, a really beautiful one. "I bought it in Pakistan," Nora smiles. "I thought it could be your photo diary ... you know, a record of your year in London."

I don't know what to say. It's a brilliant idea, of course. "Thanks," I say. I actually feel like I might start to cry so I quickly start to ask Nora what she thought about Chalk Farm. She shrugs her shoulders. "It was ... OK. It wasn't as 'wonderful' as your grandma's

+++ to puff – schnaufen +++
suspicious – argwöhnisch, misstrauisch +++
to mutter – murmeln +++ stack – Stapel +++
to be nice about sth. – etwas loben +++ to hand – geben +++

always telling you but it was a good school, I suppose. Art was the only thing I could do," she laughs.

Then she says, winking, "You know there's a boys' school right across the street?"

Hallelujah! I think. Why didn't anyone tell me before??

"Yes," grins Nora. "St Dougan's. A twin school, almost. We used to do a lot of things with them, you know, dances ..."

I'm smiling, too, now. It's the best news I've had **in ages**. It's almost as nice as the time I heard Katharina Müller had *Windpocken* and would be off school for three weeks. Ah, yes, good times.

I finally **curl up** on Nora's tiny sofa around 11, under a blanket that she bought in Guatemala. I look at the photo album she gave me, still completely empty, and try to imagine what its pages might be filled with after a year at Chalk Farm School for Girls ... which **reminds** me: I wanted to check the map of the underground to see where Chalk Farm actually is.

So I look at a **tube** map of London, something else Nora gave me this evening. It seems much more complicated, much bigger than the BVG map of Berlin. I like to think of myself as a city girl but I'm slowly realising London is a **whole** *different kind* of city.

Broughton's and Chalk Farm School for Girls are

+++ in ages – seit ewigen Zeiten +++ to curl up – sich zusammenrollen +++ to remind – erinnern +++ tube – Londoner U-Bahn +++ whole – *hier:* ganz und gar +++

near each other, on the black line, the Northern Line, Broughton's in Hampstead and Chalk Farm School nearest a stop called ... Chalk Farm, in an area of London called – guess what? – Chalk Farm, unsurprisingly.

Kreide-Bauernhof – Betti and Merle thought that was a really funny name. Then I feel bad, as I haven't **texted** them yet. I'll do it now ...

The next morning, Nora's phone rings at 6 am. The phone's on a little **carved** wooden table right next to my head so I nearly fall off the sofa.

Guess who?

"Emily! I just wanted to check that you're here ... are you here??"

Of course I'm *here*.

"Yes, Grandma."

"And you haven't forgotten that we're meeting at Broughton's today? Ten o'clock? Then they'll be waiting for you at Chalk Farm ..."

I must have fallen asleep on top of my mobile last night. My face hurts. I pass the phone over to Nora, looking grumpy in a **stripy** nightdress: "Do you *have to* call so early, Mother?"

Nora and the Queen Mother have what my mum calls a *frosty* relationship. As a child this always made me picture them having snowball fights. ***To the death.***

+++ to text – simsen +++ carved – geschnitzt +++ stripy – gestreift +++ to the death – tödlich +++

I *must* text Betti and Merle, but I'll do it later. Nora and I have to get ready quickly. It's going to be a busy day. After I've been **fitted** for a uniform, we'll meet a Miss Bardwell at the school at 1 o'clock. She'll show us around, a private tour! It's Saturday and most girls will arrive later today or tomorrow for the start of school on Monday.

I get my things together, carefully putting my new photo album in Merle's red case. Then we **stick** that in the back of Nora's **doggy** Citroen and **speed off** to Broughton's. It's not far and only takes us about ten minutes. Broughton's has been here since Roman times, probably, and was, of course, where Nora and Mum got their things for school, too.

"I used to hate the uniform," Nora says cheerfully, as she parks, too quickly, in a tiny looking space, "but, honestly, now I think it's quite … retro cool."

She's being kind. I try not to look too sadly at her Prada coat.

The Queen Mother is already standing in front of Broughton's. I haven't seen her in more than a year and she looks elegant in a tweed jacket, white hair still cut in the same **bobbed** style she's had it in *forever*. But – she's not happy.

The first thing she does when we reach her is shout, "NORA! YOU ARE 20 MINUTES LATE! CAN'T YOU EVER BE ON TIME???"

+++ to fit – anpassen +++ to stick – stecken +++ doggy – *hier:* nach Hund riechend +++ to speed off – flitzen, rasen +++ bobbed – Bob-Haarschnitt +++

The second thing she does is shake my hand. The Queen Mother never hugs or kisses anyone. She does say, warmly, "Wonderful to see you, my dear." Then she smiles and nods towards the shop.

"Come on, let's get you dressed." She gives Nora a cold look. A *frosty* look. "Do you have *time* to come with us, Nora?" Nora ignores her and we go inside.

Getting fitted for a uniform doesn't take long. I try a few things on while a kind lady **measures** me. Clothes sizes are different here, and the lady tells me I'm a British size 6 so then I just go and choose every-

+++ to measure – *hier:* abmessen +++

thing I need in a 6. The list for Broughton's is as thick as the *Gelbe Seiten* – blazer, skirt, **Wellingtons**, Macintosh sweatshirts, **cardigans**, hockey skirt – stupid, really short! – hockey socks, an awful yellow colour. They should pay *us* to buy them!

What it all *costs.* I close my eyes and try not to think what this kind of money would buy at H & M. Then, FLASH! It's Nora – taking a picture of me in my uniform with my camera, which she must have taken out of my bag. Great. Maybe I can burn the negatives.

The Queen Mother smiles proudly at me and then **utters** the words I've been waiting my whole life to hear: "I've set up an **account** in your name."

What would Betti and Merle say if they knew I had an account at a shop in London! It was always our dream, of course, to have one somewhere … *Schreiben Sie es an.*

Then I try to imagine their faces if they saw *where* I now have one. I can just hear Merle, always the optimist, saying, "Kannst du deine Oma vielleicht fragen, ob du tauschen kannst? Ich meine, Harrods gegen Broughton's? Oder vielleicht haben sie noch was anderes als Uniformen da … Accessoires? Oder DVDs?" I look around. No accessories, no DVDs. I don't think I'll **be back in a hurry**. I thank the Queen Mother and we all leave. Chalk Farm School for Girls is waiting …

+++ Wellingtons – Gummistiefel +++ cardigan – Strickjacke +++ to utter – äußern, aussprechen +++ account – Konto +++ to be back in a hurry – schnell wiederkommen +++

It'll have to wait. Nora and the Queen Mother are fighting again. Outside Broughton's. My grandma's being a Drama Queen Mother and doesn't want to get into Nora's car: "Nora ... it's *dirty*!" Nora's saying, grumpily, "It's a ten-minute drive, Mother! It won't kill you. And if it does, you'll die with your family around you ..."

Even simple things – like getting from A to B – suddenly become as difficult as those Killer-Sudoku puzzles Dad's always doing when Nora and the Queen Mother get together. I look at my watch. 12.48. We're going to be late.

Grandma's now shouting that she wants to go to Chalk Farm School by taxi. I decide to be **brave** and say firmly, "It'd be really nice if we could all go *together*," and the Queen Mother **sniffs** and finally gets into the front seat of the Citroen.

I sit in the back seat, half on top of the dog's bed, which *ugh*, is really hairy. Benjy's **obviously** a white dog ...

I stare at my legs. White dog hair on black jeans. It's a good look. Just the way I wanted to arrive at my new school.

+++ brave – mutig +++ to sniff – *hier:* schnauben +++ obvious – offensichtlich +++

Miss Bardwell's Bombshell

We drive through the area of Chalk Farm itself – no sheep, no chalk. It looks really lively, in fact, lots of nice cafés and restaurants, interesting shops. Nora **points out** a famous theatre. Suddenly everyone's much happier. And then the Queen Mother and Nora shout, at exactly the same time, "Chalk Farm School!"

I can see it, too. A large, attractive red-**brick** building, with two **distinctive** towers. I recognise it from the brochure the school sent me in Germany. (And from their Internet site, which I must have looked at a hundred times, trying to imagine myself there.) If I hadn't seen pictures of it before and I'd been by myself, I'd still have found it, as it says: CHALK FARM SCHOOL FOR GIRLS in huge letters at the top of the huge gate. Even I couldn't miss it.

But **despite** the fact it looks familiar, my heart still **skips a beat** … I'm *really* here.

"And over there," says Nora, "very important – St Dougan's! Boy Central!"

+++ bombshell – *hier:* Überraschung +++ to point out – hinweisen auf +++ brick – Ziegelstein +++ distinctive – markant +++ despite – trotz +++ to skip a beat – einen Herzschlag aussetzen +++

She points across the street and, behind some trees, I can see another similar-looking red-brick building. I even **spot** a couple of cute-looking boys, walking around in the large garden in front of the school.

The Queen Mother sniffs. "If Nora had spent *less* time thinking about boys and *more* time on the hockey field …"

Nobody's listening. We drive up to the school. The Queen Mother orders Nora to park round the back "so no one sees us". There doesn't seem to be anyone around *to* see us but Nora drives behind the school anyway.

We get out and walk slowly round to the front again. I look up at the school. It's **impressive**, no question. "The East and West Towers," Nora says. "They each have a **dormitory** in them. Your mum was in the West Tower, I was in the East. Different houses …"

Different houses. Nora and the Queen Mother look at each other, meaningfully. *Here we go again.* I've a bad feeling that someone will be sad whatever house I'm in. Secretly, of course, I like the sound of Bloomsbury more than Kensington …

Then the Queen Mother **yells** angrily, "Nora! I'm *covered* in dog hair!" and she disappears behind a large bush to try and brush her coat.

Nora **smirks.** "As if anyone will notice a bit of Benjy on her …"

+++ to spot – erkennen, wahrnehmen +++ impressive – beeindruckend +++ dormitory – Schlafsaal +++ to yell – rufen +++ to smirk – feixen, grinsen +++

"Hello!"

A voice calls out from behind us. We turn and the first thing I think is: *Wow,* a real live black-and-white photo! It's actually a woman, wearing a dark suit and white blouse, with short black hair and the darkest eyes I've ever seen on a … human. She smiles at me – wooah, *big* white teeth! – then looks at Nora. The smile and huge teeth **vanish**.

"Nora," she says in a flat voice, "Nora Millington. Welcome back."

Nora looks surprised. "Connie Bardwell? You're still here!"

I realise that my aunt and Connie were at school here together. How nice! Lovely! Old friends …

Connie Bardwell laughs. It's a dry, empty laugh.

"Well, I did go to Cambridge for five years! You … didn't study, Nora, I suppose? Not really the type, eh?"

I suddenly notice that my aunt and Connie Bardwell don't like each other. *At all.*

My aunt laughs – her laugh is much more relaxed.

"No, I didn't. This is my niece, Emily Hausmann, as I'm sure you know."

Connie Bardwell holds out her hand to me. She looks me up and down carefully.

I've the funny feeling she's trying to decide whether I'm more like my mum or the Queen Mother – *good!* – or my aunt – really *bad*. She smiles again. She looks *much* older than Nora.

+++ to vanish – verschwinden +++

"Emily from Germany! Welcome to Chalk Farm School for Girls. I'm Miss Bardwell, housemistress of Kensington. I teach Latin."

"Connie and me were at school together," says Nora, in an easy way. "Different houses, of course. Connie was *very* clever."

Nora winks at me. *Very* clever is code for – *bit of a* ***nerd***.

Suddenly the Queen Mother reappears. *"Connie!"*

Miss Bardwell's face changes at once: "Mrs Millington! How lovely to see you again!" And she hurries towards my grandma, who's smiling broadly …

"She looks happier to see Bardwell than she did to see me," **grumbles** Nora.

It's true. And then "Connie" and the Queen Mother start to talk to each other. It takes a moment. It can't be. *"Quid agis?"* I hear Miss Bardwell say in a funny voice …

"Yes," mutters Nora **grimly**. "They *are* speaking Latin to each other. Horrible, isn't it?"

It's just … *strange*. Nearly as strange as Lars-Christoph Schmid and Michael Bachmann, the two Gothic *Herr der Ringe* freaks in my class at Hermann-Hesse-Gymnasium, who chat to each other in **Elvish** all the time.

Then Nora calls out, impatiently, "Hey, Romulus and Remus! Hurryupus!" I love Nora.

+++ nerd – Streber/in +++ to grumble – brummen, murren +++ grim – grimmig +++ Elvish – Elbensprache +++

Connie Bardwell turns back to face us. She's **annoyed**. And she's **armed** and dangerous. There's a blinding flash of white light from her super-size teeth again and then … she drops her bombshell.

Though she's looking at the Queen Mother, she's aiming it at Nora and me: "I'm so very pleased that Emily is going to be in my house, in *Kensington*. It means I'll be able to take *extra special care* of her. And the family tradition is *so* important, of course."

Nora gasps. The Queen Mother looks delighted but … nervous.

And suddenly everyone is staring at *me*. Oh brother.

This is a movie I really *don't* want to be in – *Battle of the Houses II – The Next Generation?*

I don't say anything. I'm **trapped**. If I say, "Oh no!" then the Queen Mother and Miss Bardwell will go crazy. If I shout, "Oh great!" then Nora will start crying or something and, well, it's *not* really great, the thought of Miss Bardwell taking *extra special care of me.* Yuck.

Nora finally mutters, "But the family tradition could also mean Bloomsbury House, like me … Emily is a really talented photographer …"

Connie Bardwell's eyes get even darker. "Ah, of course, *photographs*. That's your job, I hear, Nora? Taking pictures at … children's birthday parties, is it? **Weddings**?"

+++ to be annoyed – verärgert sein +++ to be armed – gewappnet sein +++ to be trapped – in der Falle sitzen +++ wedding – Hochzeit +++

Nora smiles. "I have taken pictures of weddings, yes. Royal weddings, **mainly**. A few film stars."

"How … *exciting,*" says Miss Bardwell. Her big Dobermann teeth are **gritted** so hard together she can hardly speak. "But really, Nora, both Emily's mother and her grandmother were in Kensington. It was very easy to decide. Or do we have another … rebel here?"

Miss Bardwell stares at me. Dangerously.

Decision time, Emily. It's what they call a *no-brainer* in English. Here's why: I have to live with Miss Bardwell for the next year. It seems like a really bad idea to make an enemy of her before I've actually even *started* school. So I say, as happily as I can, "No, Kensington's fine. Super."

I don't care which house I'm in. **Honest**.

Nora really does care, I can tell, but she just looks at her feet. She must understand. I hope.

The Queen Mother claps her hands and nearly hugs me but then remembers that she doesn't hug people and shakes my hand instead, shouting, "Hurrah for Kensington!"

+++ mainly – hauptsächlich +++ gritted – zusammengebissen +++ honest – *hier*: ehrlich +++

For Fashion Emergencies

Miss Bardwell, now **walking on sunshine**, takes us on a tour of the school. We enter the main hall, which is beautiful, its walls covered with paintings in gold **frames**, mainly of old ladies. "Our **founders**," says Miss Bardwell. There are pretty **rugs**, some in the school colours of burgundy and yellow (OK for *rugs*, I think) and glass **cases** everywhere, full of silver cups. It feels more like a museum or a castle than a school.

Nora follows us, looking a bit miserable. She's relieved, I can tell, when her mobile phone suddenly starts to ring loudly. She has a great ring tone – the Clash song, *London Calling!* For 30 seconds, the main hall rocks! Nora runs outside quickly, talking into her phone. "Today?" I hear her say.

My eyes follow her. I'm starting to wish that I were going somewhere exciting to take lots of pictures. It's my dream, of course, to be a professional photographer …

Suddenly Nora's back again. With my things, my red

+++ to walk on sunshine – gute Laune haben +++ frame – Rahmen +++ founder – Gründer/in +++ rug – Wandteppich +++ case – Vitrine +++

case and my uniform, still in the Broughton's bags. She looks both excited and sad. "I have to go," she says quietly. "They need me in Madrid right now."

At about exactly the time that Nora says the words *Madrid right now*, it finally hits me. This isn't just a nice little trip to London to see my aunt. And I feel a bit ... nervous, to be honest. I've been looking forward to coming here for so long, I've dreamt about it nearly every night. Now I'm actually here, it's a bit scary. I can't imagine ever liking Miss Bardwell, whom I'm going to *live with*. (Suddenly I panic – surely I don't share a bedroom with her???)

Nora's shaking hands with both the Queen Mother and Miss Bardwell. "I just need a quick word with Emily," she's saying, "then she's all yours."

All yours. Oh brother.

Nora **leads** me over to a corner of the hall. We stand behind a plant, under an oil painting of an old lady. Both Nora and the old lady look very serious.

"Emily – here's a tip," says Nora quietly. "Don't cause trouble like I did. I just made things difficult for myself. The House you're in doesn't (**slight** pause) matter anyway. There'll be nice girls in Kensington, too."

Nora's whispering now. "Your grandma gives a lot of money to the school every year. That's why we're getting the private tour today. So Bard... *Miss* Bardwell

+++ to lead – führen
+++ slight – klein, leicht +++

will be nice to you. And … it'll be … fun … to learn … Latin … with her."

These words are painful for my aunt, painful.

I have to laugh. "Sure," I say, "Can't wait." Nora laughs, too. She presses an envelope into my hands. *For fashion emergencies* it says on the front. "Open it later," she says. "And just be *yourself*."

A quick kiss and she's gone. Suddenly it's just me. And the Chalk Farm School Fan Club.

Our tour of the school goes on. And on. *And on.*

The school is enormous. At first it's quite interesting to look around. All the classrooms are lovely, really big and well-equipped. The only problem is that the Queen Mother has a story about *every* room we go in, and this is driving me slowly crazy.

We see the swimming pool, the gymnasium, the library … I'm starting to think I'll spend my year in London just touring the school – *und was hast du alles Schönes in London gemacht, Emily?* – when I see it. A **darkroom**! *Darkroom* it says on the door, helpfully.

"Do you teach photography?" I say, excited. "Hmmm?" says Miss Bardwell, looking bored. "Yes, well, the Art department does. More Bloomsbury's thing, of course."

I don't care! It'll be my thing, too!

Finally it's the moment of truth and time to see – my *dorm.*

+++ darkroom – Dunkelkammer +++

Miss Bardwell says, "Emily is in the West Tower, of course. Dorm 3B," and the Queen Mother looks as if she'll cry with joy. Even the **approximately** *300* stairs we have to climb to actually *get* to the dorm can't kill her happiness. I try to imagine walking up all these stairs every day. Perhaps Grandma could give Chalk Farm School money to build a lift … The Queen Mother Memorial Elevator?

When we reach the **summit**, sorry, *top*, Miss Bardwell throws open the door, dramatically. I've got my eyes closed, I can hardly **bear** to look.

But I do, of course, and the dorm is *fine*. It looks much better than it did in the photo I saw in the brochure. Maybe it's because the sun's shining today, but it's actually a really big, light room with beautiful wooden **ceilings**. There are four beds and each has a small wardrobe next to it as well as a little bedside table and a lamp.

All the beds have cards with names on them. I try to read them. I know it's silly but I'm terrified that one might say: *Miss Bardwell*. None of them do. They say – *Melissa Kerr. Olga Petrova. Rebecca Meades.* The bed nearest the door has a card on it, which says: *Emily Hausmann*.

But – wait! The Queen Mother has actually *stopped talking* and looks disappointed, sad even. "It's all changed!" she cries.

+++ approximate – ungefähr +++ summit – Gipfel +++ to bear – ertragen +++ ceiling – Decke +++

Miss Bardwell says quickly, "It's true, Mrs Millington, we built a wall and divided your old dorm into two. This is actually one of the last bigger dorms – all the others in the main building only have two beds."

"Two!" squeaks the Queen Mother. "We had ten!"

Miss Bardwell mutters something about *fire regulations* and *girls these days wanting more* ***privacy***.

"Privacy," my grandma repeats, sitting down heavily on my bed. She says "privacy" as though it were a dirty word! *Privacy* **rocks**.

Miss Bardwell shows me the bathroom. It's right next to the bedroom and though the four sinks and the toilet are a rather **odd** avocado colour, it's fine, too. Two shower **cubicles** for four girls, though, I notice. Hmmm.

We go back into the dorm. The Queen Mother's still in a state of shock and Miss Bardwell says quickly, "A cup of tea perhaps, Mrs Millington?"

I hold my hand out to my grandmother and help her up from the bed. She's still so quiet that I'm actually wondering if she might be sick or something, she *is* 82 … Then she sees one of the name cards. "Rebecca Meades!" she says joyfully, "Mildred's granddaughter! How marvellous! Mildred and I used to bunk together, too! Let's see, it was me, Millie, Dunny, …" and she's off. Fourteen years old in her head again.

+++ privacy – Privatsphäre +++ to rock – *hier:* super sein +++ odd – seltsam +++ cubicle – Kabine +++

Miss Bardwell leads us to her **study** which is in the main building, near but – hurrah! – not *too* near the West Tower. Her study's very **bare** with nothing much in it **except** some old prints of Pompeii and a photo of a pleasant-looking man on her desk. Is there actually a Mr Bardwell????

We sit on hard chairs and drink strong tea and eat dry **shortbread**, and then Miss Bardwell talks to me about the school. It's pretty boring and all anyone *normal* needs to know: Chalk Farm School for Girls is really, really old fashioned. There are **plenty of** modern and progressive boarding schools in England. This isn't one of them.

Miss Bardwell also tells me a bit about rules and daily life, too, which is more interesting but scary. Registration is at 9 and the school day "finishes" at 3.50, though actually – *Ha!* ***Tricked*** *you!* – it doesn't, because we have "supervised prep" till 5.30 (*Hausarbeit unter Aufsicht,* we would call it back home.)

"And you can finish any homework after dinner if you don't manage it then!" Miss Bardwell says as though this were a really special **treat**!

Super!

Miss Bardwell gives me the full list of rules. I look at it quickly. *No jewellery or make-up are allowed during school hours … If pupils leave school during the week,*

+++ study – Büro +++ bare – kahl, schmucklos +++ except – außer +++ shortbread – Buttergebäck +++ plenty of – viel/e +++ to trick s.o. – jmdn. hereinlegen +++ treat – Belohnung, Vergnügen +++

uniforms must be worn … Pupils must not talk to or smile at each other …

I **made** the last one **up**. But there does seem to be a rule for pretty much *everything*.

Just then, my phone beeps loudly from my pocket to tell me I've got a new message. Miss Bardwell gives me one of her spooky **death-ray stares** and says:

"Rule number 14, Emily."

I can guess. I look anyway. 14 – *Mobile phones must not be switched on between the hours of 9 am and 6 pm and must be locked away at night.*

Miss Bardwell smiles. "This is Saturday, of course, and you *are* allowed to use phones at the weekend but from Monday …"

My *phone.* Why doesn't Chalk Farm School just **go all the way** and *cut our hands off?*

Suddenly I'm not feeling good. Really. So I say quietly, "Would it be possible for me to go and lie down? I've got a bit of a headache …"

I **make my escape**, my hands full with my timetable, the list of school rules, my Kensington house **badge** and a map of the school. I'm dreaming of just clearing my mind a bit … so much has happened today.

When I get to the dorm, I open the door. My bags have been brought up already, as if by magic. As if this were *Harry Potter* or something.

And there are two other girls in the dorm.

+++ to make sth. up – etwas erfinden +++ death-ray stare – tödlicher Blick +++ to go all the way – konsequent sein +++ to make one's escape – verschwinden +++ badge – Erkennungszeichen +++

Olga and Melissa

The two other girls don't look very happy to see me when I come in. They're lying on one of the beds, giggling at some photos. It looks like one of those scenes I saw in the school brochure, actually – pretty girls **lounging around** happily in their dorms.

One of them, a tall girl with strawberry-blonde hair a bit like Merle's, gets up quickly to shake my hand: "Melissa Kerr. Lovely to meet you. You must be Emily."

Melissa's very **well put together**, as my mum would say, in a grey trouser suit with a **plain** powder-blue shirt. It's not my style, but she looks smart.

The other girl just eyes me in a strange way from the bed. Very unfriendly. She looks great, though, in a simple black cotton dress which really highlights her beautiful platinum-blonde hair – *natural* platinum-blonde hair, I would say.

"This is Olga," says Melissa.

Olga says nothing.

"Right," I **mumble**. There's a long silence. I feel I

+++ to lounge around – herumliegen +++ to be well put together – gut angezogen sein +++ plain – einfarbig, schlicht +++ to mumble – murmeln +++

should add something else, so I begin, "I'm from Berlin …" Then I stop talking.

I've just noticed that Melissa has already unpacked and I can't believe it … *she has a picture of a horse in a large silver frame on her bedside table.*

Melissa follows my **gaze**, reaches for the photo and hands it to me, looking proud. "That's Almonds. A beauty, eh?"

I stare at the photo. Almonds looks … well, big. Brown. What else can one say about a horse? I've never met anyone who *owned* a horse before. Horses were circus animals in Berlin …

"Cool," I say. "He looks … really cool."

Melissa puts the photo back on her bedside table and tells me that it's her third year at Chalk Farm School for Girls – we're all in the third **form** – and *it's OK here,* she says, looking at Almonds a bit sadly. Melissa's **from the Home Counties**, Bucks or somewhere I've never heard of: "Just up the road."

I don't really understand this. "Why do you **board** here if you don't live so far away?" I ask.

"Oh, Mummy and Daddy … travel a lot," Melissa says vaguely.

I notice there are no pictures of her parents next to her bed. "My brother goes to St Dougan's, though," Melissa says, her face brightening.

She points to a photo of a boy of about 16 which is

+++ gaze – Blick +++ form – Klasse, Jahrgangsstufe +++ to be from the Home Counties – aus der Gegend von London sein +++ to board – *hier:* wohnen +++

also on her bedside table. It's much smaller than the one of Almonds and partly hidden behind it.

Olga still hasn't opened her mouth. She's just watching me, really closely. I'm *sure* she's looking at my hairy jeans. What's her *problem* with hairy jeans exactly? Maybe she's allergic to dogs or something … Time to find out, I decide.

A little nervously I ask, "Where are you from, Olga?"

Olga seems surprised, as though I were a servant girl speaking to her, the Queen of the Dorm, without permission. But she does at least answer, "Florida."

"Olga's daddy's a **billionaire**!" squeals Melissa. She puts her hands over her mouth. "Sorry, Olga …"

+++ billionaire – Milliardär +++

"No, he's not," says Olga drily. "Not yet."

"I bet you miss the weather in Florida," I begin, but Olga cuts me off.

"Daddy asked for a *double room* this year," she **hisses** to Melissa, looking meaningfully at me. "But the school said no. Sharing a bigger room **encourages** …"

"Traditional **values**!" finishes Melissa and they both laugh, Olga a little bitterly. This is obviously a Chalk Farm in-joke.

"It would have been wonderful if it were *just the two of us,* darling," Olga **snarls**. Then she picks up one of the photos she and Melissa were looking at when I came in and says, turning her back to me, "And this is us **scuba diving** …"

I can **take a hint**. I let Olga and Melissa get back to looking at what seem to be pictures of Olga's holiday, spent on her father's yacht in the **Crimea**. Olga's family's originally from Russia, I would guess, from her name and her accent.

Anyway, who needs photos of beautiful people on yachts when you've got a timetable to look at. And such a good one. The week gets off to a *fantastic* start – double Latin with Miss Bardwell, followed by Sport. (I quickly calculate – we have *four hours* a week of sport!) Lunch, then it's double Maths and, finally, the only thing of the day which sounds OK, English Literature …

+++ to hiss – zischen +++ to encourage – stärken +++ value – Wert +++ to snarl – knurren +++ scuba diving – Tauchen +++ to take a hint – einen Wink verstehen +++ Crimea – Krim +++

I should have been reading more in English in my summer holidays before coming here, instead of wasting time thinking about Sebastian. *Sebastian*. It was a bit stupid of me to bring his picture here. Perhaps I should just get it out to throw it away. Make a fresh start …

I'd better unpack anyway. I'm suddenly a bit ashamed of my brown paper bags from Broughton's. I open my red case first and take out the big envelope of photos in it … Mum and Dad. Betti and Merle at Popkomm. There he is … Seb…

Woosh! The photo's gone, **snatched** out of my hands by Melissa, who' s now standing behind me.

"Cute! Is this your boyfriend back home?" she giggles.

"No," I say, confused. "He's just a … friend. Can I have it back, please?"

But Melissa's passed the photo – Sebastian just after finishing the 400 metres last year, in shorts! – to Olga, who's looking at it with interest.

"Mmm," she purrs. "Nice legs."

"He's just a friend," I mumble. "Really." I'm bright red but I **sense** that both girls, especially Olga, are more interested in me now.

"Olga has a boyfriend, too!" laughs Melissa, giving me the photo back. "Olga, show her!"

I want to say again that Sebastian's not my boyfriend but I don't. I'm curious about the photo

+++ to snatch – schnappen +++ to sense – spüren +++

that Olga's getting from the **drawer** of her bedside table.

"Taki," she finally mutters, holding out a picture of her and a boy who must be about 20. He's very **handsome** and very **tanned** and, no surprise, very rich-looking, a massive gold watch on the arm that he has hanging over Olga's shoulder. She's not smiling in the picture, I notice.

"Nice," I say. "Have you been going out with him for long?"

"Eight months," **replies** Olga. She gives the photo a strange look. "He's in Florida."

"I've just got Almonds to **cuddle**!" laughs Melissa. It's a big **horsey** laugh.

She looks **tenderly** at the photo of Almonds again and then turns to me as though she has just had an idea of *genius.*

"Oh. My. Goodness. I've just thought of something – *you're* German – *Almonds* is German, too!"

"Almonds is *German???*" I say.

"Yes, a Bavarian warmblood! Daddy had him shipped over from Munich!"

I don't reply. I can't reply.

But there's no stopping Melissa: "Oh, this is *too* good! I'm just going to call Almonds now and tell him!"

I'm not making this up.

+++ drawer – Schublade +++ handsome – gut aussehend +++ tanned – gebräunt +++ to reply – erwidern +++ to cuddle – knuddeln, kuscheln +++ horsey – pferdenärrisch +++ tender – zärtlich +++

Melissa **speed-dials** a number on her mobile and then starts to talk in a funny babyish voice. "Are they looking after you, OK? Mummy misses you, darling ..."

She must have called her stables or something and someone's holding the phone to the horse's ear, I suppose – either that or she's a ***lunatic***.

And then she passes the phone to me: "Say something in German to him. He'll love it."

What else can I do? I sigh, take the phone and say, "Hi, Mandeln, wie geht's? Alles klar bei dir?"

Heavy breathing.

"He's fine," I say to Melissa, giving her the phone back.

Olga actually looks amused.

As Melissa continues to giggle with the love of her life, I try to think about unpacking again but then remember I have to check the text message I got in Miss Bardwell's study. I get my phone out.

It's from Betti – *UND????* is all it says.

There's only one possible answer: *Notfall. Alle spinnen hier. Rette mich.*

+++ to speed-dial – schnell wählen +++ lunatic – Verrückte/r, Irre/r +++ as – während +++

Beef Olives

But there's no escape from the **madness**, no rescue party from Berlin. The door of our dorm opens and closes as fast as the Queen Mother's mouth.

Firstly, it's the school **janitor** with Olga's luggage. Olga has about 40 cases – the sweet smell of designer leather now fills our dorm. The janitor looks like he's about to have a heart attack as he leaves. Olga doesn't even thank him for nearly killing himself.

Another knock at the door. It's the Queen Mother.

"Oh *good*!" she says when she sees Olga and Melissa. "You've made friends already!"

Olga rolls her eyes.

"Are you Millie's granddaughter?" the Queen Mother asks Olga, **eagerly**. Olga looks horrified and I say quickly, "This is *Olga*, Grandma."

The Queen Mother stares at Melissa, hopefully. Melissa shakes her head and says gently, "You must mean Rebecca … she's not here yet."

The Queen Mother looks a bit disappointed about

+++ beef olives – eine Art Roulade +++ madness – Wahnsinn +++ janitor – Hausmeister +++ eager – begierig, eifrig +++

this but she's had a fantastic time, I can tell. She says goodbye and invites me to her house – The Grange or "Millington Palace" as Dad likes to call it – for half-term, the school holidays in six weeks.

Out and in. Next it's Miss Bardwell to "check on things". She, too, seems jolly. She obviously loves Melissa and Olga. They answer politely when she asks them about their summer holidays, but when she leaves, it's clear they *don't* love her.

"Another year of her **breathing down our necks**," mutters Olga …

"Maybe this year she'll actually get married and leave!" laughs Melissa.

Get married? I think about the photo on Miss Bardwell's desk. I suddenly remember that she did have a ring on, a small diamond one. But who'd want to *marry* Miss Bardwell? Imagine waking up to those *teeth* every day … **My blood runs cold** at the thought.

"She's **engaged**," says Melissa excitedly. "To one of the teachers at St Dougan's, Mr Michaels … and guess what? They've been engaged for *eleven* years!!!"

Eleven years … that's nearly my lifetime. *Someone's* not in a hurry.

I finally get unpacked, which actually takes about 90 seconds as I don't have much stuff. I try not to look over at Olga, who's pulling an endless series of beauti-

+++ to breathe down s.o.'s neck – jmdm. im Nacken sitzen +++
My blood runs cold. – Es läuft mir eiskalt den Rücken herunter. +++
to be engaged – verlobt sein +++

ful and expensive designer outfits from her beautiful and expensive suitcases and throwing them carelessly into her wardrobe.

"I'm hungry," says Melissa suddenly to Olga. "Shall we risk it?"

She obviously means dinner, which I'm curious about. I'm hungry, too.

Melissa smiles kindly at me. "Do you want to come to eat with us?"

I glance quickly at Olga. She looks as if she couldn't care less whether I came with them or *died*, so we go downstairs together.

Once in the dining hall, I see that quite a few other girls have already arrived – we have to queue up to get dinner. I look at the menu board while we wait: "*Saturday – British Classics Day – Beef olives.*" Yummy, I think. **Beef** and olives, sounds nice.

And then I get served.

We studied a bit of philosophy back at Hermann-Hesse. You know, when is a chair not a chair and all that. Well, here's a question: when is an olive not an olive? Answer: when it's in a beef olive.

They're *disgusting*. **Tough** meat wrapped around something **mushy** and mysterious in the centre, certainly not an olive. It's dog food – *for people who hate dogs.*

"It's called an olive because of the shape," says Melissa helpfully. She sees my face. "It's not always this

+++ beef – Rindfleisch +++ tough – *hier:* zäh +++ mushy – breiig +++

bad. They only cook traditional British recipes once a week. Very popular with the …"

"Parents," says Olga, darkly.

"And on Tuesdays and Thursdays we actually have a choice!" says Melissa brightly. She even **swallows** some of the "food", unlike Olga who just looks tortured. I wonder what she eats back home in Florida – caviar with fries?

Personally, I could **murder** a Currywurst.

Back upstairs again, I'm still hungry and not really sure what to do with myself. I'm tired and to be honest, I'd love to go to bed but I decide it's too early – a bit uncool. Not as uncool as having a picture of a horse next to your bed, but still. I'm just deciding to go and check my e-mails in one of the computer rooms in the main building when I realise Olga and Melissa are talking about how much pocket money they get.

I can't help it – I listen.

"My mothers says 100 will just have to do me this term," Melissa's saying, in a depressed voice.

"100," mutters Olga. "Is she *crazy*?"

100 a month doesn't seem too much. More than me …

"100 pounds *a week*," repeats Melissa, **desperately**. "How on earth's a girl supposed to manage?"

I nearly fall onto my bed. 100 a week?? That's 150 euros!!!

+++ to swallow – schlucken +++ to murder – *hier:* verdrücken +++ desperate – verzweifelt +++

I actually feel like crying. Mum's going to transfer me my money every month. I now have *30 pounds* left until October. I think angrily about the price of the coffee at the airport when I was waiting for ... *Nora.* I suddenly remember the envelope she gave me earlier.

For fashion emergencies. I'd nearly forgotten about it, in all the day's drama. It's still in the pocket of my jeans and I get it out and open it, just to see ...

There are *300 pounds* in the envelope – six new 50-pound notes. I look at them. I could kiss the Queen's face. I could kiss Nora. I look up at the sky, where she probably is right now, my angel auntie, winging her way to Madrid. *Thanks.*

Lights out is at ten. Another rule. But tonight I don't care. By 10.02 I'm fast asleep.

It's so quiet here. That's the first thing I notice when I wake up. In Berlin, our flat is right on a busy road – it's loud and dirty and crazy. Here, you almost jump when a leaf falls from a tree. BOO!

We're in central London. They *say*. But when I look out of my window, I don't see a breathtaking panorama of Big Ben or the Houses of Parliament or the Tower of London or anything. All I can see is the huge sports field and **loads of** trees (without leaves). The school grounds are so big, the school's almost its own country. The **Posh** People's Republic of Chalk Farm School.

+++ loads of – eine Menge +++ posh – nobel, piekfein +++

It's Sunday and so only one day left before we start classes. Rebecca, the fourth girl in our dorm and the Queen Mother's old friend Mildred's granddaughter, arrives.

I had high hopes for Rebecca. Olga and Melissa are obviously best friends and it'd be nice if Rebecca could be someone for me. Maybe a rock fan or really into art …

But this is Kensington House, of course, so "Rebecca" isn't even a "Rebecca". She **introduces herself** as "Becks" and **pumps** my hand energetically.

Becks like the beer? Like David Beckham???

No, Becks is short for Rebecca, it seems. Becks is jolly, loud and a *sports fanatic*. She seems to have the strength of ten men and doesn't need a janitor to bring her luggage up, even though she easily has the same amount as Olga. Lots of sports equipment – tennis rackets, hockey sticks, **goal posts**, a table-tennis table, a rugby pitch (three of these things were not true).

I spend the rest of Sunday hiding in the school library, flicking through English books and trying not to worry about …

+++ to introduce oneself – sich vorstellen +++ to pump – quetschen +++ goal post – Torpfosten +++

From Dawn till Dusk

Monday morning! It's soon clear that, like a mouse in an experiment, my new life will be controlled by bells. The first one rings at 7.15 – the "rising bell". I get up. I rise. It's time. Time to put my uniform on **properly**. I look fearfully at my wardrobe, then get it out, watching the other girls throw theirs on casually. *Uniform Profis.*

My hands are actually shaking so hard that Melissa has to help me with my tie. When I'm completely dressed, I look in the mirror. Hmmm. I'm certainly not a "retro cool" style icon but I don't want to throw myself out of the window either. I am *really* glad that no one from Hermann-Hesse can see me now, though. Betti and Merle have already begged for a photo of me in my uniform – no way!

The breakfast bell rings at 8.25, so we all go down together to the dining hall and eat. Then another bell rings – it's telling us to go to assembly, apparently. Assembly is when the whole school **gathers together** to "meet, sing and give thanks", I seem to remember

+++ dawn – Morgengrauen +++ dusk – Abenddämmerung +++ proper – korrekt +++ to gather together – sich versammeln +++

reading in the school brochure. We all march off, like robots on their way to meet their robot leader …

Mrs Randall. Mrs Randall is our headmistress. "She's always got mad hats!" whispers Melissa as we enter the assembly hall. I spot her and her hat at once. She's a slightly younger – 79, maybe? – version of the Queen Mother really, and she's wearing a **peach**-coloured dress and … a hat that looks like it has a dead **squirrel** on it. *Mad.*

Mrs Randall makes a short speech to welcome us to our new year at Chalk Farm School! As I half-listen, I look at all the rows of girls. Chalk Farm School has about 700 pupils and it's funny to see them all sitting together in their identical uniforms. For a moment I think: Mum's right. Wearing a uniform does make you feel a *bit* like being part of a big team … Or **sect**.

Then Mrs Randall finishes talking and it's time to sing the Chalk Farm School for Girls song. Yes, really – their own song. The only lines I remember are:

And we shall do our best
From dawn till dusk.
We shall not rest
Till we have served
Our school.
From dawn till dusk.

Now that *is* a bit scary.

+++ peach – Pfirsich +++ squirrel – Eichhörnchen +++ sect – Sekte +++

And then – the fun really starts. Latin with Miss Bardwell.

It's no wonder "Connie's" so friendly with the Queen Mother – they can both talk for Britain. Miss Bardwell goes on and on about it being *a new school year with new chances to improve! And we have a new girl! Introduce yourself please, Emily? Emily? Emily????*

I suddenly realise she means *me*.

I groan inside but get to my feet. "Hi," I say. "I'm from Germany. I live in Berlin and …"

"Emily is *bilingual*, girls!" interrupts Miss Bardwell. "I sometimes wish I'd grown up bilingually – in Latin and English. But I'm a bit young for that, of course!"

She laughs, far too loudly, at her own joke. I don't laugh. Firstly, because it's not funny. And secondly, a golden rule at Hermann-Hesse, funny or not, it's uncool to laugh at teachers' jokes.

I look around the room quickly, trying to spot anyone who *is* laughing – one of my world-famous *Schleimer* tests. I notice that Olga's staring at Miss Bardwell as though she were **insane**, Melissa' s smiling politely.

There's one girl, very pretty, with blue eyes – one of which looks a bit **swollen** – laughing as though she's in a comedy club and having the best night of her life.

"Does anyone have any questions for Emily?" smiles Miss Bardwell when the swollen-eyed *Schleimer* has finally stopped laughing.

+++ insane – geisteskrank +++ swollen – geschwollen +++

One girl wearing glasses puts her hand up. Somebody sighs and Miss Bardwell says, a bit **wearily**, "Sadie?"

"Did you see the wall come down?" asks Sadie.

"The wall?" I repeat.

Sadie-with-glasses **nods**. "The Berlin Wall? Did you see it come down?"

Did I see *the Wall* come down? How old do I look?

"No," I mutter slowly, "I wasn't … born."

Then the swollen-eyed-laughing-*Schleimer*-girl says quickly, "Sadie, *everyone* knows that the Berlin Wall fell in 1989 and that East Germany was officially **dissolved** the following year."

Actually, I don't think *anyone* else here knows that, but Miss Bardwell smiles again and says, "Excellent, Amanda!"

Sadie seems a bit sad. "Sorry," she mumbles to me. "I didn't mean that you look … *old* or anything."

Amanda laughs loudly again. It *echoes*. It reminds me of someone …

As she laughs, I hear a loud clear beep: one other thing I remembered to bring with me from Berlin, luckily. My super-sensitive *Zickenradar*. Amanda will have to be watched.

The first week is OK, on the whole. I survive.

A couple of the teachers are a bit boring – well, they

+++ weary – lustlos, matt +++ to nod – nicken +++
to dissolve – auflösen +++

are *teachers* – but none seem **evil** or anything. None of them are Herr Eisenhardt.

Nicest of them all is Miss Shaw who teaches art. I talk to her a bit about photography and she smiles when I ask her about the darkroom: "You don't have a digital camera? We don't use the darkroom much any more. Most girls aren't interested."

My camera isn't digital but I have a true connection with it. I've tried out Nora's new state-of-the-art ones but my old one just *feels* better. I love waiting to see how photos will look – like opening a great present. Unfortunately, there aren't many "great presents" to look forward to opening yet. The only things I've taken pictures of so far are our school buildings. The architecture of our school is interesting, a bit Gothic, with its **haunted** castle-style towers. But it's still, you know, *architecture* and not cute boys or anything *exciting*.

Anyway, thank goodness there is no one taking any photos of the only real *nightmare* of Week One which is, surprise, surprise, sport. My first lesson is actually OK – we don't do much except some warm-up exercises. I'm actually starting to think sport here might not be too bad when we have our next lesson …

Hockey time! I don't even know the rules. No one cares: Becks is our team captain and tells me quickly that I'm to "defend" in today's game. With Olga, who, it's clear, *hates* hockey …

… and *hates* our goalkeeper, Babs Deeds. Babs is a

+++ evil – böse +++ haunted – spukig +++

friend of Becks and another sports freak. She's wearing a scary-looking goalkeeper's mask which hides most of her face but not the fact that she *really* wants to win today.

To top it all, it's *raining*. The wind is **howling**. It's freezing. Our tiny, silly hockey skirts are awful. I'm actually even happy about the yellow socks – thanks to them, I still have some feeling in my legs. The only nice thing about this is that Olga, who usually ignores me, actually talks. Maybe it's a bit like when people stuck in lifts together tell each other their life stories because they think they're going to die.

"I can't believe I could be on the beach in Saint Petersburg right now," Olga sighs, as we watch our

+++ to howl – heulen +++

team hitting the ball around at the other end of the pitch. We're playing against Knightsbridge and – hurrah! – we're better than them, so there's not much for Olga and me to do yet.

Olga's sighing about Saint Petersburg, *Florida*, apparently. I didn't even know there was one. She tells me that her family moved from the Russian Saint Petersburg to the American one ten years ago. She feels more American than Russian now …

"You could be walking along the sand with Taki," I say dreamily. I can see them both. Beautiful people, living beautiful lives. Beautiful *warm* lives.

Olga throws me an odd look. "Yes," she says quickly, "with Taki." I'm dying to know more about Taki. But that's all I get.

Olga does tell me, shouting above the sound of the rain, that it was her father's idea to send her to an English school. "He loves England," she says, looking miserably at the clouds above us, as black as Miss Bardwell's stare when you get something wrong in Latin. Or when *I* get something wrong.

From up at the Knightsbridge goal, I hear a voice scream, "NO!" It's Amanda, the swollen-eyed *Schleimer*. I've just noticed that she's wearing a bright green helmet today. She's now holding her hands up to her face, looking scared. Then Olga laughs. It's not a nice laugh. "Poor **Cyclops**," she **sneers**. "Amanda, see her? She got hit in the eye by a ball in the first form – she

+++ Cyclops – Zyklop +++ to sneer – spöttisch lächeln +++

nearly went blind. She won't play hockey without that stupid thing on her head ... and she's really terrified of being hit again ..."

Just as I'm feeling a bit sorry for Amanda – *Cyclops, that's just* ***mean!*** – more tragedy and disaster. While we've been talking, nearly all the players on the field have started to head our way – a horde of wet psychopaths. I feel like running back to Germany, but it's too late. The only things now standing between the horde of wet psychopaths and victory are Babs Deeds, Olga and me. It's our big moment.

Olga is absolutely ready for it. She smiles and steps to one side, almost politely, to let Knightsbridge's

+++ mean – gemein +++

strikers past. Brilliant. Babs screams something at her that I don't understand, but which is probably, "I'll kill you, Olga!"

I panic and put my stick out and close my eyes … it's useless. *I'm* useless. Knightsbridge score: GOAL! I can hear the sound of cheering … I open my eyes slowly. Just in time to see Babs Deeds marching towards Olga and me. In her serial killer/goalkeeper mask.

Babs looks as though she's in the **mood** to do two things: 1) **rip** Olga's head from her shoulders and hit it hard across the field with her hockey stick, 2) have a quick cup of tea and a biscuit and do the same to me. She could, honestly, no problem.

Well, one problem. Like most people, I've noticed, Babs is actually a bit scared of Olga. It's hard to explain why and has a lot to do with the way Olga *stares* at you. Right now, she's just *staring* at Babs, smiling … Babs returns to the goal, grumbling, leaving Olga's perfect head where it should be.

Olga's quite cool, I decide. Maybe we could really be friends. If we live long enough.

But later Olga ignores me when I wave to her in the dining hall. And back in the dorm, when I try to talk to her there, she acts like she can't remember having met me before.

Olga – the human **cryptogram**. I can't work her out.

+++ striker – Stürmer/in +++ mood – Stimmung, Laune +++ to rip – reißen +++ cryptogram – Rätsel +++

Hier ist überhaupt nichts los

At the end of my second week at Chalk Farm School, Miss Bardwell stops me in the corridor and says, "I promised your grandmother I'd write her a letter to tell how you're getting on. Shall we do it together? Thursday afternoon in my office?"

"Fine," I say. And then, as I walk to my next class, English Literature, I wonder – how *am* I getting on?

I haven't had much time to think about it. And that, in a way, is the problem. So much has happened – but so little of it's been exciting.

School itself is fine. There's just *so much of it.* It's nice to start a bit later in the morning than we did in Germany, but I miss getting out at 3 and going somewhere else. By the time we've finished with "supervised prep" in the evening, I'm too tired to do anything except eat and go to bed. And when I wake up in the morning, I'm already in school. *From dawn to dusk*, the school song said. It really is. *Nightmare.*

It would all be fine if I had found someone to have a laugh with, but I haven't made any real friends yet. There are a couple of girls in our class who look like they might be slightly cool. But, well, anyone cool already has friends and anyone who isn't cool – well, who wants to be friends with them?

I look around the class now. Everyone is concentrating hard, writing things down, actually listening to Amanda, who's reading aloud a **speech** from "Othello" by William Shakespeare. Unbelievable. They're so serious, these girls. They seem to worry about things like exams and what university they will go to all the time. Nobody seems to want to have … *fun*.

Maybe there's more *fun* in other houses. The Bloomsbury girls really do look cooler, but we never see much of them. And whenever I do meet anyone who's not from our house, it's clear that saying you're in Kensington is the same as wearing a T-shirt which says, *I'm totally boring. Please don't talk to me.*

What would make life MUCH more interesting, of course, is having *boys* around. They drove me crazy, too – I think of lovely Sebastian wasting his lovely time on *you know who* – but at least we had a laugh with them. At least they gave me something to look at … *the back of that neck …*

When I finally go to Miss Bardwell's office to write my "report" for the Queen Mother, I don't tell her any of this, of course. I just say quietly that I'm enjoying everything, but it's **lies**, all lies:

It's official – I'm definitely homesick. Boysick.

+++ speech – Rede, Monolog +++ lie – Lüge +++

Chalk Farm School for Girls rule 34 – *Girls who have any personal problems should see their* ***guidance teachers*** *for help*. Miss Bardwell is my guidance teacher. No chance.

As Nora has spent exactly *one day* in London since I arrived here – she's in Morocco this week – and is therefore *no help*, the only person I can really tell about how bad I'm feeling is my mum, on the phone.

Mum is **sympathetic** but she also says those annoying things that Mums say: about *giving things a chance, it taking time to* ***settle in****, about being patient. You've just arrived, Emily!*

But she's worried enough to offer to come and visit me when I call her that weekend. "We could just hop on a plane," she says lightly as though this were *easy*. My mum *hates* flying. *HOP ON A PLANE = CARRIED ONTO PLANE BY MY DAD, SCREAMING NO NO NO NO NO NO.*

I know Mum would do it, for me. But I still say, "NO." It's expensive and she has to work and, whisper it, *I don't want to have* ***failed*** *at being in London by myself.*

Hier ist überhaupt nichts los. That's what I told Betti and Merle, in one of my e-mails to Berlin. I miss them; I wear my "Berlin loves you, Emily" T-shirt most nights to bed. I sometimes wonder if Betti and Merle even read *my* mails – they're *soooo* boring. No jokes,

+++ guidance teacher – *etwa*: Vertrauenslehrer
+++ to be sympathetic – Mitleid haben +++ to settle in – *hier:* sich eingewöhnen, einleben +++ to fail – versagen +++

no action. My only news has been things like the fact that it was Almonds' birthday last week. (Melissa actually made a cake and then forced me to sing "*Hoch soll er leben!*" down the phone.) That's the "news" from London ...

The news from Berlin, on the other hand, is always exciting. The biggest stories from there so far have been ...

Gothic Lars-Christoph Schmid is in love with Betti – "*und hat mir ein Liebesgedicht geschrieben. Auf Elbisch. Zumindest glaub ich, dass es ein Liebesgedicht war ... hab eigentlich kein Wort verstanden.*"

The owner of Mondstein asked why I don't come for *Milchkaffee* any more.

Merle thinks she has a crush on a boy in the *zehnte Klasse* but isn't sure.

Betti and Merle are both saving like crazy to come and visit me here. LONDON SPARFONDS: 13 EURO UND 47 CENT!

Those are what I call real news stories!!

It's great that Betti and Merle e-mail me so often ... it's just a shame that *someone else* in Berlin doesn't e-mail me every now and then. And I don't mean Herr Eisenhardt.

Sebastian. I haven't heard a word from him. *Funkstille.* He's obviously too busy chasing Katharina Müller to have even noticed that I'm gone. And I can't bring myself to e-mail him. I *can't.*

The best thing to do would be to forget him. Fall in

love with someone else. But who?? There's not exactly a big choice. The only boys I've seen up close in the past month or so have been 1) our male teachers (teachers = not boys) 2) our school janitor, Mr Lee (aged **approx.** 78) 3) the **bin men**, who collect the school rubbish every Monday.

Of course there are *hundreds* of good-looking boys, living about 800 metres away from me. It's just cruel: St Dougan's is right across the street but it might as well be St Dougan's School for **Martians**. It's *another planet.*

Nora said that the boys and girls schools actually *did* things together but so far there has been no sign of us doing *anything* with them. There's nothing to look forward to …

And then, like a **beam** of light at the end of a beef olive filled tunnel, there *is* something to look forward to.

The beam of light appears in assembly. It's a surprising place for it to appear: I *hate* assembly. Every Monday the whole school meets together and our head-teacher Mrs Randall wears a mad hat and tells us what will happen to us this week. That we will play hockey *from dawn till dusk*, usually.

This morning something's going on. I notice it even as I'm taking my seat in the assembly hall. The girls

+++ approximately (approx.) – ungefähr +++ bin man – Müllmann +++ Martian – Marsmensch +++ beam – Strahl +++

around me are all excited. There's lots of whispering and elbowing each other and pointing at the stage where the teachers and Mrs Randall sit. And then I see it. The cause of the excitement.

It's unbelievable. It can't be true.

I can't believe my eyes.

It's a BOY.

Here! In our school! I'm confused ... maybe someone should call the police or something! Perhaps he's lost. ACROSS THE STREET, SIR! I feel like shouting. YOU'RE IN THE WRONG SCHOOL!

I'm a bit **short of breath**, actually. It's not just any old boy **stranded** here. It's a beautiful, blonde-haired one. Tall, too, his long legs are stretched out in front of him. He looks **adorable** in the black and red St Dougan's uniform. *Adorable.*

He's sitting, nodding seriously, as Mrs Randall – is that a *baby panda* on her hat today? – talks about the importance of making sure that paper **towels** actually go *in* the toilet bins after we've washed our hands.

Then – *finally!* – Mrs Randall gives us all a big smile. She knows. She can feel it – the adrenaline in the room. "And now, girls," she **booms**. "Ed Stanton from St Dougan's School for Boys is going to give us some exciting news about our social programme."

Ed Stanton gets to his feet. He looks relaxed – he even looks like he's going to enjoy speaking to 700 girls

+++ to be short of breath – außer Atem sein +++ stranded – *hier:* mittellos, hilflos +++ adorable – anbetungswürdig +++ towel – Handtuch +++ to boom – dröhnen +++

who are all staring at him like he's a ***gift*** *from heaven.* I mean, which boy *wouldn't* enjoy that?

"Good morning, Ladies", he says, in a flirty way.

There's a SIGH in the room that nearly lifts the roof.

Ed Stanton tells us that we are all invited to come to a disco and a concert at St Dougan's in two weeks. "The concert part is my band playing," he says proudly. "We started it a few months ago and it was our music teacher's idea to let you hear a few of our songs. Anyway, I'll be hanging up a poster after assembly with all the details. See you all there, I hope!"

He flashes his killer smile at us and a girl next to me looks like she really will die.

Another teacher stands up to talk about a History trip to the Museum of ... but this time it's not just me who's not listening. Everyone is still just **gazing** in wonder at Ed Stanton, who's now sitting back in his seat, still smiling.

+++ gift – Geschenk +++ to gaze – schauen, starren +++

Not Only My Destiny

I always thought that those "love at first sight" stories you sometimes read in bad magazines were unbelievably **lame**. You know the kind of thing: I-realised after-3.4-seconds-that-we-would-get-married-and-have-seven-children-and-live-happily-ever-after-in-Baden-Wuerttemberg-forever type stories. I *hate* those. Falling in love takes time. I took *three years* to realise that I was in love with Sebastian, for instance. That's nearly a quarter of my life!

But now **the joke's on me**. I've actually fallen in love at first sight! Telegramme for Mr Ed Stanton: *Let's get married and live in Baden Wuerttemberg forever! (We can talk about the seven children part.)*

Ed just has … an aura, something so special. I can't even begin to describe it. So I won't. Just trust me – he's *amazing*. If you'd been there, you'd have fallen in love with him, too.

I know it in my bones – Ed Stanton is my destiny. I *feel* it. I'm sure.

+++ destiny – Schicksal +++ lame – lahm, wenig überzeugend +++ the joke's on me – *etwa*: es hat mich erwischt +++

Until about 20 minutes later, when I hear Amanda say, "Ed Stanton is my destiny. I can *feel* it."

This amazing, tragic coincidence happens after Ed Stanton has left the assembly hall, **chased** by about 400 sweating, **panting** girls. He has the concert poster rolled up in his hand. He walks casually over to the notice board in the main hall, hangs the poster up, turns, waves and leaves. Gone.

One girl actually starts *crying*.

The rest of us look at the poster as though it were a **holy relic**. Here's what it says:

+++ to chase – jagen +++ to pant – keuchen +++ holy relic – heilige Reliquie +++

THE KITTY GAGARINS LIVE!
DISCO AND CONCERT
AT ST DOUGAN'S BOYS' SCHOOL
OCTOBER 15th, 8 pm.
ALL PUPILS OF CHALK FARM SCHOOL FOR
GIRLS WELCOME!!!

It has a cool picture on it, too, one of a cat dressed in a **spacesuit**, waving from a Soviet-style space rocket. There's also a photo of four cute boys, all holding instruments. Ed Stanton has a guitar. He's a guitarist!

There are now about 20 of us still staring at the poster. Some of us seem to be **praying** that the poster will turn into an Ed Stanton hologram or something. It doesn't. Some girls finally give up and leave. Not me. I'm standing behind Moira, a girl in the year above us who's in a **wheelchair** and I still can't take my eyes off the poster. Moira also hasn't moved for about ten minutes.

It's just then I hear someone say, "Hey, Moira! Do you mind? You've been parked there for *hours*. Do they even *have* wheelchair **access** at St Dougan's?" It's Amanda. Of course.

"Shut your face, Cyclops!" hisses Moira, but she **wheels** to the side. *Cyclops*. I mustn't laugh.

Amanda looks furious for a moment and obviously thinks about saying something else to Moira but

+++ spacesuit – Raumanzug +++ to pray – beten +++ wheelchair – Rollstuhl +++ access – Zugang +++ to wheel – rollen +++

changes her mind. Instead she turns to talk to one of her "friends". Amanda doesn't really **do "friends"**, I have the feeling. She does "strategic partners". One of them, a girl in our class called Laurie, is standing with her now.

Amanda's smiling. "There he is again. Look, Laurie. Laurie, *there*." (Laurie, I later discover, needs glasses but won't wear them and is allergic to contact lenses.)

Laurie **squints** at the poster. "Oh right, I think I can just … Which one is he?"

Amanda rolls her eyes. "Oh Laurie! He just spoke to us, like *five minutes ago?*" And then Amanda starts talking about how she first saw Ed play rugby a few weeks ago. How she just knew then he was *the one:* "Ed Stanton is my destiny. I can *feel* it." I gasp.

"Hi, Emily," **trills** Melissa suddenly. "You excited about the concert, too?"

Bad timing. Melissa has just joined the crowd **worshipping** at the **shrine** of Ed Stanton.

"Hi," I **grunt**. Not now: I'm really trying to listen to what Amanda's saying. How is it possible that we like the same boy? It isn't right. It's *unnatural*. And she knows him, I think miserably. She *knows* him.

I've got Melissa talking to me in one ear, something about her brother Josh. I'm smiling but really, only my *other* ear is actually switched on. The one listening to

+++ to change one's mind – seine Meinung ändern +++ to do friends – *etwa*: sich Freunde machen +++ to squint – schielen +++ to trill – trällern +++ to worship – huldigen +++ shrine – Schrein +++ to grunt – grunzen +++

Amanda, who's now telling Laurie that Ed is "totally into her" and that she's sure – she *knows* – that they'll get together at the concert.

"It's our night. He said he'd see me there. He's *sooooo* mine," Amanda says, **pompously**. Then she gives me a quick, suspicious look with her evil eye and off she goes.

Amanda's destiny. Right. She saw him first. And she is really pretty. If you don't look at her eyes for too long. But if anyone in "Emily Hausmann's Destiny Department" is actually reading this, I just have one question: why do the boys who I like always prefer Superzicke? Perhaps I should start being nasty to people in wheelchairs, then the boys would go crazy for me, right? What's wrong with them?

Anyway, I'll just have to try and forget about Ed. *Forget him. Forget him.*

I try really hard. I go to my classes that afternoon. I listen carefully. I write things down. I read books. I eat dinner.

I don't forget about him. I do a really silly thing instead. I go back to the notice board later that evening. I look carefully around me to check that no one is watching and I rip the Kitty Gagarins poster down and stick it carefully in the rucksack I've brought with me.

I *need* that poster. And everyone knows about the concert already anyway. It's all anyone is talking about.

+++ pompous – pompös +++

Official Wardrobe Crisis Number One

The next two weeks before the concert are boring. My photo diary stays pretty empty. All it has in it so far: my pictures of us all at the TV Tower in Berlin, me in Fitzrovia and at Broughton's with Nora, some shots of the school buildings. Oh, and some photos of the *worst Saturday of my life,* last weekend, when I was stupid enough to agree to go to London Zoo with Becks and some of her friends. Babs Deeds was there and maybe I'm paranoid but I'm *sure* she tried to push me in front of a bus at one point. Babs Deeds hates me.

The 14 days before the concert are *not only* boring: they're also bittersweet. Sweet = the **prospect** of actually seeing the band and my lovely boy. Bitter = the thought of such a lovely boy being Amanda's *destiny*.

Still, the fact that Ed and Amanda are engaged or whatever doesn't stop me from wanting to look nice for the concert. There will be *700* other boys there. Ha! They can't all have a *Superzicke* fetish.

I've been really, really good so far and haven't

+++ prospect – Aussicht +++ still – *hier:* dennoch +++

touched Nora's money. This is my first real wardrobe crisis. I must be strong. I know what Nora would want me to do.

I get the envelope she gave me from the drawer of my bedside table. I've put my Kitty Gagarins poster there, too, and I look at Ed's face tenderly. *Ed. Ed ... oh, stop it.* I shut the drawer and off I go to Chalk Farm underground station.

It's the first time I've been out of school by myself and it's a great thing to do. Here I am, out on the tube, in my normal clothes, looking at normal people. I feel really free. I should worry less and do this more often. **After all**, I said I wanted to be more independent in

+++ after all – schließlich, immerhin +++

London. There are fantastic art galleries waiting for me, interesting buildings. The Tate Modern. I want to see the **Gherkin** …

But today, I've got *fashion,* not art or architecture, on my mind. I've a clear **destination**, too: clothes Mecca. Top Shop at Oxford Circus, Britain's largest fashion store.

It's so big I find it easily. I go inside and *wow!* It's amazing, huge. A cathedral of clothes! They even have an in-store DJ. The shop is full of girls my age, all *ooing and aahing* and praying for miracles to happen inside their **purses**.

I've got 100 pounds with me. I go first to the racks of T-shirts, of course, and find five or six I really like. I finally choose one that has a photograph of **bolts of lightning** on the front. It's nice, but I don't know. I feel like something a bit … different.

And so I look at the dresses. I don't really wear dresses. I'm famous for *living* in my jeans. But, by myself, I can look at things I wouldn't normally. Then I see it …

Bright red, with a thin white belt round the middle. It has some white zigzag **stitching**, really simple, round the **collar**. It's very 1960s. It's very classic. It's *the one.* I look at the price tag: *please let it be less than a hundred pounds …*

+++ gherkin – Gurke (*hier:* ein wegen seiner Form so genanntes Gebäude in London) +++ destination – Ziel +++ purse – Geldbörse +++ bolt of lightning – Blitz +++ stitching – Naht +++ collar – Kragen +++

Yes! It's 80!

Though Berlin is about 900 km away, I hear my father scream **in agony**. All the girls in the shop freeze. The DJ stops playing music. Traffic comes to a halt outside …

Not really. The T-shirt is 20 pounds. I can get both things, makes a nice, round *Hunni.* I won't have any money left for anything, not even a drink for the way back but I've got a return ticket and *it's the dress destiny wants me to wear for the* **gig**, I can feel it! I pay, bravely, and head back to school.

Destiny. There's that word again.

Back in the dorm later, I'm not sorry I bought my new outfit. Everyone's getting very dressed up, even Becks. It's the first time I've seen her not wearing her **tracksuit** at the weekend. Tonight she's got a purple **rara skirt** and a T-shirt saying: *Hockey players do it better!* She's tried.

"They have a first-class rugby team at St Dougan's," says Becks excitedly, putting on too much pink lipstick. As it's Saturday, we are actually allowed to wear make-up. (I've put on a bit of very dry mascara I brought from Berlin. Plus a tiny bit of eye liner. Oh, and a **smudge** of lipgloss and **blusher**. Nothing. Totally natural.)

Olga *really* isn't wearing make-up. She doesn't need

+++ in agony – qualvoll +++ gig – Auftritt +++ tracksuit – Jogginganzug +++ rara skirt – Rüschenrock +++ smudge – *hier:* Hauch +++ blusher – Rouge +++

it – she is **superhumanly** beautiful. She's taken her usual 30 seconds to get ready and looks amazing in a simple grey, suspiciously Armani-looking dress. She's now eyeing me in my red dress. I *know* what she's going to say: *Did your grandmother make that outfit, Emily? Or maybe your nine-year-old brother?*

But she doesn't. She surprises me once again by actually saying, "You look nice." I have the feeling *she means it.*

I pack my camera – finally something really worth taking pictures of tonight! Then we all make our way downstairs to the main hall where Miss Bardwell and some of the other housemistresses are waiting for us. Our guards for the night – they march us out of the door. I'm surprised they're not carrying Kalashnikovs.

Outside, in the cold of the evening, I **shiver** in my little red dress. I can't be as cold as Amanda, whom I spot walking ahead of me, wearing a *tiny* **sequined** blue **playsuit**. She looks good – **apart from** the pair of sunglasses she's got sitting on her head: it's October in London, not summer in Ibiza. *Sunglasses.* **Dumb.**

Then it's through the gates of St Dougan's we go, up the path ... **My heart's in my throat.** I'm so nervous! Ed's here! And he must be nervous, too ... about the concert and meeting the girl of his dreams again ...

Once we're inside St Dougan's, I can't help it. I start

+++ superhuman – übermenschlich +++ to shiver – frösteln +++ sequined – paillettenbesetzt +++ playsuit – kurzes Höschen +++ apart from – außer +++ dumb – doof +++ My heart's in my throat. – Das Herz klopft mir bis zum Hals. +++

to feel really silly, really **giggly**. I'm not the only one … Most of the girls and boys look as though they've been given laughing gas. It's a bit like being at a human zoo; each group is staring at the other like they were something exotic.

I'm standing laughing with Melissa when I notice Miss Bardwell talking to a man who looks familiar. "Her **fiancé**, Mr Michaels," whispers Melissa. "Check out the body language."

Mr Michaels and Miss Bardwell are standing about three metres apart from each other. *Intimate*. I wonder if she speaks to *him* in Latin. *Amo, amas, amat* and all that?

We hang around in the main hall of St Dougan's for a while before we're *finally* lead into the assembly hall. It's been decorated in a bright, slightly children's birthday party kind of way. *Far too many* balloons. The lights are *far too* bright as well. I look around the room, **blinking** in the **harsh** light. Maybe Amanda was right to bring sunglasses …

There she is, Amanda, already positioned right in front of the stage, Laurie next to her. Amanda's now wearing her sunglasses. (I have a nasty thought – maybe she doesn't want Ed to see her big eye?) Melissa, Becks and Olga are standing near the back of the hall

+++ giggly – albern +++
fiancé(e) – der/dieVerlobte +++
to blink – blinzeln +++ harsh – *hier:* grell +++

with a tall boy of about 16, whom I recognise from the photo by Melissa's bed as her brother, Josh.

I go over and join them. Melissa introduces me to Josh, who, it must be said, is better-looking than his picture. He gives me a quick smile. He seems a bit nervous, actually. So does Becks. She's talking, too fast and for reasons no one understands, about golf. Olga just looks bored, of course, and is rolling her eyes at Becks.

Then the music starts! It's an old Britpop song: *Girls and Boys*. Perfect! Josh smiles. "Shall we dance?" he says. He's talking to Melissa and Olga, I think, but Becks shouts, "YES PLEASE!" grabs him by the arm and drags him onto the floor. Josh looks terrified. Melissa and Olga **burst out laughing**. Melissa hurries over to rescue her brother by dancing with him, too. Olga just stands there, smiling, watching the three of them carefully.

I want to dance as well. I've got my camera with me, though, and am not really sure what to do with it. Maybe Olga would look after it? When I ask her, she answers me with a look that says: *Are you mad*? I do feel a bit mad. *Disco fever*. I give her a look back that says, *Please?* and finally she nods and takes my camera.

I head towards the dance floor …

It's quickly clear that Becks is a *terrible* dancer. She tries far too hard as though there were points or goals

+++ to burst out laughing – in Gelächter ausbrechen +++

to be scored. She's sweating heavily and keeps dancing in front of Josh, who keeps moving away. He's trying to concentrate on Melissa. They both move in the same way, like they share a **gene** for dancing. Sweet.

It's fun, this, the first real fun I've had in ages. Watching everyone is **hilarious. I can't help but** notice that all the girls are dancing with the girls and the boys are dancing with the boys! They're scared of each other! Crazy!

I'm so busy laughing and dancing that I've actually even nearly forgotten how scared *I* am about seeing Ed again. I remember when the DJ stops the music and says, "And now St Dougan's is proud to bring you … The Kitty Gagarins!" Oh! Everyone turns to look at the stage.

The curtains open, slowly and not very smoothly, to **reveal** four boys, all with instruments and smiling nervously. One of them, a handsome guy of about 16, standing behind a microphone – the singer? – waves and says, "Hi, this is our first ever gig so … be kind!"

Standing behind him: *Ed Stanton.* Looking even more handsome out of his school uniform. He has a great Bob Dylan T-shirt on, real vintage, I'm sure of it.

Above the noise of the band's opening **chords**, I think I hear Amanda (and at least 50 other girls) groan. It's a cover version – the song, not the groan – *London Calling* by The Clash! (Nora's favourite song!)

+++ gene – Gen +++ hilarious – lustig +++ I can't help but … – Ich kann nicht anders, als … +++ to reveal – enthüllen +++ chord – Akkord +++

It's clear at once: no one has to be kind to the Kitty Gagarins. They *rock*. They totally rock.

Quite a crowd has already joined Amanda and Laurie in front of the stage. Becks and Melissa are now there, too. And all the girls and boys are *finally* mixing. I must get my camera and take some photos, quick! The lead singer looks a bit like one of those boys from Leeds that Merle liked so much last summer. I'll take a few pictures for her and post them – *einer dieser Jungs als Briefsendung*. That'll make her laugh.

I try to find Olga. It's not hard – she's the only girl in the room ignoring the band. She's standing at the side of the hall, deep in conversation with Josh, who's probably the only *boy* in the room ignoring the band. When I reach them and shout, "MY CAMERA?" Olga looks annoyed. It's hanging over her shoulder and she takes it off and pushes it into my hands, **roughly**. I'm in too much of a hurry to get back to the band to care.

I **muscle** my way to the front of the crowd – standing on Amanda's toe as I do so. She looks at me through her sunglasses. Her left eye gets bigger when she's angry about something, I've noticed before. I can't see it but I **bet** it's HUGE now.

But, do you know what? I don't mind. Because I've just met *someone else's* eye. Here's a clue – *someone else* is playing the guitar. *Someone else* is a brilliant guitarist.

+++ rough – *hier:* grob +++ to muscle – drängeln +++ to bet – wetten +++

Oh my. Sometimes, at home in Berlin, my brother Max used to **bounce** on my **chest** when I was lying on the floor reading or something. I feel the same way now, breathless, like someone has just used my stomach as a trampoline. *Wow*.

+++ to bounce – hüpfen +++ chest – Brust(korb) +++

Too Cool for School

I'm so nervous, I almost feel like running away back to the no-boy-zone safety of Chalk Farm School for Girls. Ed *is* smiling at me, I'm sure of it. Or maybe it's just at my camera.

I wish Betti were here, she always knows for sure if a boy's really interested in you or not. Even without her "Test" – she can smell it.

Ed's probably smiling at everyone … Destiny's Child/Amanda, for instance. I think he even gives her a little wave at one point. Oh well.

At least I'll get some cool pictures tonight. I take lots more. I shoot the rest of the band, too. They're all cute, actually, especially the drummer, who has big glasses that somehow manage to stay on his face as he bangs away. But my heart definitely belongs to Ed …

The Kitty Gagarins play some of their own original songs. One's called *Where the Girls Are* and is obviously about our school. It's really funny. They do lots of cover versions and these are all amazing, too.

I'm already wondering how quickly I can get to the darkroom to get my photos developed. Two days at least, two whole days! I take my phone out and shoot a couple of quick pictures with that, too, so I'll have something to look at before then. *I will survive!*

It's a great night. The crowd go crazy when the Kitty Gagarins say goodnight and, after making us sweat and panic for a few minutes, they return for one more song. "This will be our first single," says the lead singer, grinning. "It's called *Too Cool for School*." Everyone cheers.

Their first single? Is he serious? Maybe the band will be famous and I can tell my grandchildren I was at their **debut concert** ...

Too Cool for School is funky, really **catchy**. We're all singing it by the end: *I don't like your rules and we're too cool for school!*

Then it's all over. The Kitty Gagarins leave, waving at ... all of us? (Does the guitarist wave at *me*? *Does he??*) Amanda's still standing where she has been all night, looking up at the stage, a bit desperately. She's actually taken her sunglasses off as though she can't quite believe what hasn't happened to her tonight. She waves at Ed and calls his name. Either he doesn't hear or ... he isn't interested. I'm actually becoming *pretty sure* it's the second possibility ...

She and Laurie are now the last ones left standing in front of the stage. "He'll come over now," I hear her say to her strategic partner, in a worried voice. But Ed doesn't come over. And Amanda's **running out of**

+++ debut concert – Premiere +++ catchy – eingängig +++

time – the girls are being **rounded up**. It's time for us to leave St Dougan's. No one looks like they want to, even Miss Bardwell, who has bright pink **cheeks** and actually gives Mr Michaels a little kiss goodbye! It was that kind of night.

Most of us run back to Chalk Farm School. It's freezing now, and we're all totally underdressed. I manage to turn my head and take one last look back at the boy's school. *When will I be here again? And more importantly, when will I see Ed again?*

Back in the warmth of the dorm, everyone discusses the evening excitedly. Actually, *everyone* really means Melissa and Becks. Olga just lies on her bed, doing her Sphinx **impersonation**, and I can't say much because I'm still in shock. I can't believe it. I'm really honestly pretty sure that the guitarist was looking at me. A *lot.*

Becks, it's clear, didn't notice the band much. She only had eyes for … *Josh*. Oh dear. She seems to **have a crush on** him. A big one. She's still red in the face and keeps repeating herself about *what a great dancer Josh is! Melissa, he must lift weights, right? He doesn't have a girlfriend right now, am I right, Melissa? Melissa?*

Melissa doesn't answer. She looks a bit worried and changes the subject quickly: "What did you think of the band, Emily?"

"They were cosmic," I sigh.

+++ to run out of time – keine Zeit mehr haben +++ to round up – zusammentrommeln +++ cheek – Wange +++ impersonation – Personifikation +++ to have a crush on s.o. – auf jmdn. stehen +++

I'm actually wishing for the first time ever that I had a digital camera! I could be looking at the guitarist right now. The photos on my phone are rubbish – all bad light and the backs of heads. There's *one* of Ed that is … *alright*, but I have to lock my phone away now anyway.

What happens next is silly, but I'm in love, remember? It's a silly feeling, love, so I give the photo of Ed on my phone a tiny quick kiss. In the bathroom, where no one can see me. *Goodnight, my sweet rock-and-roll prince!*

Sunday is the longest day of my life. Not really. It is, in fact, the longest day of *anyone's* life, *ever*. I'm not allowed to use the darkroom by myself (even though I *can*!) and I have to wait for Monday and Miss Shaw to be there before I can develop the photos from the concert.

Miss Shaw is already looking at her watch as we go into the darkroom. It's after five and she obviously wants to get home. She's young and pretty and looks like she has a life **beyond** Chalk Farm School for Girls. "You can do this yourself," she says. "I'll just wait to see how the first photo turns out and then I'll go."

We set up the **trays** and the **developing fluid** and then … the guitarist's face appears in black and white. And my face goes bright red.

+++ beyond – jenseits von +++ tray – *hier:* Wanne +++ developing fluid – Entwicklerflüssigkeit +++

Miss Shaw laughs. “Now I understand the interest in photography, Emily!” Off she goes, still laughing, leaving me, still blushing, to get on with it.

I develop all of the photos. A few are a bit **unsteady** (I was too nervous!) but on the whole, if I say so myself, they’re pretty good. I’m excited.

And then later, when I’m showing the photos to Melissa in the dorm, I have a bit of luck. When Melissa sees one of the pictures of Ed, she says, “Oh, yes, Josh knows him. What’s his name again ... Ted, was it?”

“Ed,” I mutter, casually. “I *think*.”

+++ unsteady – verwackelt +++

Melissa smiles. "He seems to be looking at you in a lot of these pictures."

It's true. It's really true. Amanda's destiny, ha! Amanda's worst nightmare, more like! And Josh knows him … we have a *connection*.

Suddenly life at Chalk Farm School feels fantastic. Birds sing. Flowers bloom. Well, no, because it's October but hope now **colours** everything. The hope of meeting Ed again. I watch the St Dougan's boys walk past our school, scanning for that head of blonde hair. I look at my photos every day. I **keep the faith**.

My luck is still in on Thursday night. We're all in the dorm, getting ready for bed. I'm lying on mine already, reading a music magazine and imagining a conversation with Ed. I'm also trying to ignore Becks, grunting like a pig as she does her 50 nightly sit-ups next to me. *Twenty-uhuhuh-seven … uhu … Twenty …*

Melissa's brushing her teeth in the bathroom. Suddenly she sticks her head round the door, electric toothbrush still in mouth. (Melissa *always* brushes for *hours*. I only brush for hours on "British Classics" evening – to kill the taste.)

She takes the toothbrush out. "Oh, **by the way**, Emily," she says, "I told Josh *(Becks stops in mid-sit-up: Thi…)* that those photos you took were great. And he told Ted? Ed? The guy from the band? Anyway, he

+++ to colour – bunt färben +++ to keep the faith – an etwas glauben +++ by the way – übrigens +++

remembered you and asked if he could get your number. He'd really like to see your pictures."

Oh *man*. I could kiss Melissa **right on the spot**. But I won't. I'd get an electric toothbrush in the eye.

Instead I mumble, a bit nervously, "Sure, he can see them. You can give him my number."

"Oh fine," says Melissa vaguely. "Actually, I already did. Sorry, knew you wouldn't mind."

"How is Josh?" says Becks, interrupting. "Is he ...?"

Melissa sticks her toothbrush back into her mouth and disappears quickly into the bathroom.

+++ right on the spot – auf der Stelle +++

Zwei neue Nachrichten

I'm excited all day Friday about getting a text from Ed. It's almost *painful* to lock my phone away as usual in the morning.

My brain is on answering machine: *Hi, Emily's brain's not here right now but if you'd like to leave a message, she'll call you back in a week.* Miss Bardwell leaves a message: WAKE UP AND CONCENTRATE!!!! I don't care. My only goal in life right now is to get upstairs to the dorm again and check my *real* messages on my *real* phone …

Finally it's 6 pm and the **torture** of supervised prep is over. I run, perhaps faster than I have ever run in my life, upstairs. Turn key, get phone – ***steady,*** *hands, steady!* – take deep breath.

My phone still has its German settings. *Zwei neue Nachrichten,* it says …

One is from Mum. The other is from a new number. It must be … It is.

Hi Ed from KGs here. RU photo girl in cte red dress? Wnt to show me ur pics sometime?

+++ torture – Folter +++ steady – ruhig +++

I think quickly. I'm not really good at **text speak** in English but *R U* – Are you? *Wnt* – want. *Cte* – cute! I reply at once.

No probs. When and Where? Emily.

He said I had a cute dress! (I *knew* that 80 pounds was an investment.)

Ten minutes pass. 20 minutes. 22 minutes and 37 seconds ... I'm *dying*. Maybe I was too direct? Perhaps I should text Betti to ask for advice but if I use my phone to text her then Ed can't text *me*.

Melissa comes into the dorm and wants to ask me something about a photo, I think, but I can't really follow her. *Come on, phone! Come on, baby! You can do it!*

"Are you ... OK?" says Melissa finally, after I've asked her to repeat everything for the 20th time.

"Pardon?" I say.

BEEP! A new message ...

Tom. At 5? School gates. CU Ed.

Tomorrow ... see you ...

Cool I reply.

I manage to say, "I'm *great!*" to a confused Melissa and collapse onto my bed.

It's really happened. I can't believe it. I read and re-read the message ... I've got a date! A date TOMORROW with the best-looking boy I've ever seen and the most talented ...

Rule Britannia! Viva Chalk Farm! And Sebastian ... *who????*

+++ text speak – SMS-Sprache +++ Rule Britannia! – *etwa*: Es lebe Britannien!

Bei Thienemann von Joanna Thompson
in der Reihe »Freche Mädchen – Easy English!«
ebenfalls erschienen:

Girls' School – *The Ed Affair*

Thompson, Joanna:
Girls' School – England Calling
ISBN 978 3 522 50016 6

Reihengestaltung und Gesamtausstattung: Birgit Schössow
Innentypografie: Marlis Killermann
Schrift: Minion und LTT Tapeside
Satz: KCS GmbH, Buchholz/Hamburg
Reproduktion: immedia 23, Stuttgart
Druck und Bindung: Friedrich Pustet, Regensburg

5 4 3 2 1° 09 10 11 12

www.thienemann.de
www.frechemaedchen.de